Wrestling with Writing

Wrestling with Writing

Instructional Strategies for Struggling Students

Nicholas D. Young, Bryan Thors Noonan,
and Kristen Bonanno-Sotiropoulos

ROWMAN & LITTLEFIELD
Lanham • Boulder • New York • London

Published by Rowman & Littlefield
A wholly owned subsidiary of The Rowman & Littlefield Publishing Group, Inc.
4501 Forbes Boulevard, Suite 200, Lanham, Maryland 20706
www.rowman.com

Unit A, Whitacre Mews, 26–34 Stannary Street, London SE11 4AB

British Library Cataloguing in Publication Information Available

Library of Congress Cataloging-in-Publication Data Available
ISBN 978-1-4758-3881-7 (cloth : alk. paper)
ISBN 978-1-4758-3882-4 (pbk. : alk. paper)
ISBN 978-1-4758-3883-1 (electronic)

∞™ The paper used in this publication meets the minimum requirements of
American National Standard for Information Sciences—Permanence of Paper
for Printed Library Materials, ANSI/NISO Z39.48–1992.

Printed in the United States of America

Nicholas D. Young

With deep respect and admiration, I would like to dedicate my contributions to this book to my second-grade teacher, Miss Rose Knight. Miss Knight had a long and distinguished career as a dedicated teacher at Alstead Elementary School located in Alstead, New Hampshire. She was one of those rare teachers who knew the importance of holding students accountable whether or not they wanted her to do so at the time. As the years have passed, I have gained a deeper appreciation for her style and commitment to high academic standards. Miss Knight, please know that your contributions to education were far from forgotten.

Bryan Thors Noonan

I dedicate my contribution to this book to Corey Wright and Zeina Spaulding for their support and commitment to shaping me as a teacher. I was fresh off the street as a reporter when you both entrusted me to design the newspaper team and writing classes at our school. You always made sure my students had what they needed, and your encouragement gave us all inspiration to succeed.

Kristen L. Bonanno-Sotiropoulos

I would like to dedicate this book to my grandmother, Philomena Price. You have shown me what it means to be a strong, independent, and confident woman. You were always there when I needed you most—to protect, support, and encourage me. With your unwavering love, I know I can aspire to anything I put my mind to. "Ti voglio bene nonna."

Contents

Foreword

The time has come to view writing from a different stance, one in which the role of the educator is at the heart of the instructional equation. Since the writing revolution of the 1970s, to a now steady decline in writing scores since 1998, policymakers and educators alike are concerned (Teachers College Reading and Writing Project, 2016). This current writing crisis in our schools calls for a complete overhaul of how we have taught writing, and even more how we, as educators, have thought about ourselves as writers.

Educators must first be willing to explore and understand their own writer's identity. This, similar to one's own personal identity, is comprised of thoughts and feelings about the act of writing, memories about writing from childhood, and experiences we've had while reading books written by authors we appreciate or dislike. These elements contribute to a writing identity that everyone poses. Educators must learn to deeply explore this identity piece of their students before tackling the daunting task of being an instructor of writing. In addition, educators must accept and use their strengths as a writer, and be able to admit weaknesses and seek development.

With educators at the center of the writing instruction, certain habits of mind need to be embraced. One such habit is to develop a personal writing identity as well as of the students in their charge. At its most basic level, this can be done by collecting wondrous words and tantalizing phrases from all genres of text, and creating personal writer's notebooks in which to store them for sharing (Ray, 2015). It is through adopting practices such as this one, and many others, that an educator builds the confidence necessary to grapple with writing instruction.

The instructional equation necessary to create student writers should consist of educators who are given strong preservice and continued in-service training in how to teach writing; student-directed learning opportunities; and a standards-based, rigorous curriculum. As daunting as this task may seem, it is important to consider why writing is important and how to teach the craft of writing, as well as what supports are available when formulating a solution.

Writing is important for a myriad of reasons. It provides an outlet for students who need to be heard and affords them some creative freedom, while building their academic stamina and developing perseverance. Writing is also a core skill needed for students to navigate through many of life's tasks, be it presenting facts about something specific, defending an opinion, or sharing a personal story. Writing transcends further than students sometimes think, such as college applications or into the hands of future employers, and as such educators need to constantly stress how writing can become a powerful tool.

Moreover, writing can be seen as the great equalizer among many students (Calkins, 2016). Those who struggle most, from the Special Education and English Language Learner populations, can feel empowered when it comes to writing within the poetry genre that often requires fewer words and is more condensed by nature. The most reluctant writers can thrive when allowing them time to sketch/label what they intend to write, and talk through their ideas with a writing partner first (Calkins, 2016).

Writing is also important as it bears such weight with state assessments. Success in classrooms across America is measured using those very same exams that require students to be writers in all content areas. The recently revised Massachusetts Curriculum Framework for English Language Arts and Literacy has added sections entitled "Connections to the Standards for Mathematical Practice" and "The Massachusetts Writing Standards in Action" that highlight the importance of this vital task (Massachusetts Department of Elementary and Secondary Education, 2017).

With this in mind, educators need to learn to teach writing differently than ever before, adopting a mind shift from acting as keeper of the knowledge to facilitator of the learning. This includes being responsive wherever students are in their trajectory and knowledgeable about how children develop into writers (National Center for Education Statistics, 2012). It is through this repositioning of the educator that the importance of teaching writing as a craft can become the focus.

Educators should teach the craft of writing by encouraging students to listen to, read, and discuss exemplars every day as a pathway to producing stronger writers. Students need to hear rich language, unique sentence structure, and interesting writing styles in order to transfer those attributes into their own work. Peer conferences, guided writing groups, and interactive online tutorials are other strategies that provide necessary feedback for students' production and improvement. There is a direct correlation between the amount a person reads and the writing skills they possess; therefore, independent reading time (IRT) should be held as one of the most sacred blocks in the instructional day (Hanski, 2014).

Through the use of mentor texts, educators can help students develop a "consciousness of craft" (Calkins, 2016), which is the ability to replicate great techniques they've seen. Students also need to spend time working through the formal writing process in a workshop setting. The Teachers College Reading and Writing Project's (2016) research base advocates for:

- teacher leads **brief** periods of explicit instruction
- teacher demonstrates **habits** of good writers
- teacher **models** using the skill/strategy in context for students to follow
- teacher pauses to make thinking visible to the students **(think aloud)**
- teacher debriefs to **name** each step of the strategy

It is through models such as this that struggling students can make considerable strides toward becoming successful writers.

Continuous modeling for students as adult writers is another method of teaching writing as a craft. Students need and want to see the productive struggle that educators go through in order to remain motivated and inspirited; thus, it is pertinent to remain current in writing content, in order to be able to produce exemplars for student use (Vermont Writing Collaborative, 2017a). Whether it is through anchor charting or providing personalized feedback in student notebooks, educators must be able to hone in on specific areas of growth, as well as provide the commentary and examples for improvement.

With the educator as guide and the student as lead, a focus on differentiated supports is essential to further develop the craft of writing. Structure in both physical environment, as noted earlier, and on the written page is paramount. When students are asked to articulate what helps them to be successful in school, their responses are inevitably: stability, consistency, and routine, which are all part of structure (Keene, 2012). It is vital, therefore, that within the writing process, the educator provides time, choice, and ownership to ensure solid Common Core State Standards instruction (Keene, 2012).

Educator development is perhaps the single most influential factor toward improved student writing. Students become better writers when educators have an arsenal of tools to pull from as supports. Thus, frequent and ongoing professional development opportunities where techniques can be seen in action and where new tools are explained and time is given to investigate are essential components (National Writing Project, 2017). For this reason, investing in developing teachers as writers first will ensure that our students reap the benefits later.

This suggests our immediate work is with educators, or, better yet, with entire schools to learn how to support each other in cultivating building-wide writing communities (Vermont Writing Collaborative, 2017a). If writing is at the epicenter of a school's culture, true growth in both students and educators will occur. The learning site may then be seen as its own think tank capitalizing on the strengths of educators already on the premises. In recognizing how the educator must remain at the center of the instructional equation, development should be provided in a variety of formats and cater to all learning styles.

A strong emphasis should be placed on educators learning from each other (Vermont Writing Collaborative, 2017a). Regular visits to other classrooms and even partner schools can be a catalyst for self-improvement. Educators agree that they learn the most from being able to watch each other's best practices live. This, along with clear and regular professional development in strategy instruction and content knowledge, will help educators become more equipped to lift the level of their students' writing (National Writing Project, 2017).

It is crucial to remember a few key points as we view writing from this new stance with the role of the educator at the heart of the instructional equation. First, educators need to immerse themselves in discovering their writing identity. This, along with strong professional development in how to teach the craft of writing, will help educators grow exponentially. Next, students need self-directed learning opportunities whenever feasible. Educators should offer guidance in creating writing goals, for example, but then allow students to self-regulate their work, providing choice and voice in all assignments. Finally, content knowledge must be kept current, with educators solely focused on learning from standards-based resources and materials.

On a personal note, it's been through my eighteen-year career in education that I have come to understand how professional development, specifically, can directly impact teacher motivation as a means to improving student outcomes. I have been fortunate to receive professional development from Harvard University Graduate School of Education, the International Literacy Association, and the Vermont Writing Collaborative such that I have come to know what works and how to get that information to educators. I have learned that when educators feel as if they are an investment, change will come. Educators need to see writing as a way they can grow in their craft as teacher and facilitator, not just as another content area to check off while lesson planning.

It is my hope that you will take time to pause for reflection as you read through the chapters, taking a moment to open yourself to the possibilities that come with new learning. Contemplate about what change will come from your research that can directly impact the students in your care. Make a decision to put one new thing into practice today. Specifically, make note of something that can be done to develop your writer's identity and make you a more valuable asset to your school community. Lastly, consider one small change that could make the biggest difference in your teaching. When all this is said and done, you will truly be wrestling with writing for the win.

Melanie Kornacki
District Literacy Coach
Springfield Public Schools, Springfield, Massachusetts

Preface

Promoting high-quality writing instruction is of utmost importance. With the adoption of the Common Core State Standards, the emphasis on written expression is at the forefront of all academic domains. Written expression is used to measure student achievement, gain acceptance into postsecondary settings, and be successful in one's career.

In an effort to promote high-quality writing instruction for all ability levels of students, educators must arm themselves with the tools and knowledge necessary to ensure this endeavor. The importance of developing writers, the writing process, the use of evidence-based writing strategies, and the importance of the role that professional development plays in supporting the teaching and learning of writing development are all discussed in this book.

Wrestling with Writing: Instructional Strategies for Struggling Students is designed to be a valuable resource for all educators who seek to gain a better understanding of writing development, effective writing teaching practices, and meeting the instructional needs of struggling writers. Educators will gain a thorough understanding of the importance of developing proficient writers and how to do so effectively as well as benefitting from the extensive research provided in this book.

The motivation for writing this book comes from several concerns:

- *Our belief that proficiency in written expression is essential for college and career readiness;*
- *Our knowledge that approximately 74 percent of children in this country write below the proficiency level (National Center for Education Statistics, 2012);*
- *Our awareness that students who struggle with writing can reach proficiency through consistent and effective teaching strategies;*
- *Our commitment to encouraging all students to see the value and experience the creative pleasures writing has to offer; and*

- *Our confidence that efforts to encourage proficiency in written expression in all students must extend beyond the classroom door, and incorporate collaborative efforts with families, peers, and other educators.*

Chapter 1 introduces the reader to evidence-based practices. Evidence-based instructional practices are defined in terms of what they are and the criteria used to identify them. The Individuals with Disabilities Improvement Act of 2004 (IDEIA) as well as the Every Student Succeeds Act of 2015 (ESSA) place an emphasis on improved student outcomes. Both acts accentuate the use of evidence-based instructional practices (Cook & Cook, 2013; Graham, Harris, & Chambers, 2016). In addition, the setting of high academic standards and pressure to improve student outcomes, in all academic areas, including written expression, combined with a wide range of student ability levels, makes the implementation of evidence-based instructional practices not only necessary but required (Samuels, 2016).

Evidence-based writing practices for struggling students and those with learning disabilities are the focus for chapter 2. The Common Core State Standards require that all students are proficient in written expression. Writing skills are critical to pass high-stakes testing as well as a requirement for graduation (Flanagan & Bouck, 2015). According to the National Center for Education Statistics (2012) it is estimated that only 27 percent of students in grades 8 and 12 are proficient or higher in writing and an alarming 74 percent are below the proficiency level (Harris & Graham, 2013). Specific writing practices are presented in order to expose the reader to highly researched strategies to use with their classrooms.

Professional development is a critical topic within teaching and learning, and chapter 3 examines the issue carefully as it pertains to writing. Effective professional development has been proven effective at supporting high-quality teaching instruction and increasing student achievement; however, not all professional development opportunities are valuable. We identify the critical components required to ensure successful professional development.

Chapter 4 takes the reader through the writing pyramid. The writing pyramid is a framework of supported instructions for students who may struggle with the writing process. This tiered approach helps students navigate through the five principles of sound writing: thinking, planning, structuring, editing, and revising. In addition, this framework moves students through three levels of learning: the creative writing tier promotes thinking and free expression; the argumentative writing tier teaches students how to structure those original, creative thoughts into opinions about issues relevant to modern life; and finally, the Research-Based Writing tier helps the student take a wider berth around those same issues by offering unbiased, inclusive evidence while connecting these issues to personal opinions and society as a whole.

The development of self-regulation skills and their importance within the writing process is discussed in chapter 5. Writing instruction must begin with universal principles that work in every writing situation: engagement, self-efficacy, reflections on skills, the foundation of grammar, and learning to be a critical reader. These principles are the foundations of all writing situations, even when the expectations of final outcomes change. Development of these principles allows writers to self-regulate throughout the writing process.

Struggling writers often lack a depth of knowledge or life experience to draw on while writing; thus, chapter 6 looks closely at prewriting activities and their utmost importance in writing development. It is essential to use brainstorming techniques that expose students to examples of quality writing. The prewriting stage must be introduced as imaginative and open thinking, which in turn allows the struggling writer to feel empowered by the writing process. Prewriting activities develop the struggling writer by giving time and focus on how to generate ideas, plan content, then study how that preparation builds into drafting an effective essay (Graham, McKeown, Kiuhara, & Harris, 2012; Graham & Sandmel, 2011).

Chapter 7 stresses the importance of effective writing structure instruction. Students struggle to learn the fundamentals of written structure if the components of a clear, unified sentence have not been mastered (Hudson, 2016). Teaching the components of a masterful sentence is essential to being able to guide the struggling writer to layer those same ideas in a coherent and organized fashion that makes up the structure of a paragraph and then a longer piece of written work.

The authors examine effective ways of supporting the editing process in chapter 8. Editing strategies provide the struggling writer ways to identify and resolve any deficits that occur during the writing process. While writing, students must focus attention on the following: generating new information, structuring the information available, and rereading and refining text that is already written. Teacher feedback, peer reviews, instruction in goals and strategies, and providing evaluation criteria are a few ways to increase competency in revision skills and overall writing quality (MacArthur, 2016). Revision techniques assist students with self-regulation throughout the writing process (Graham, Harris, & McKeown, 2013; Graham, McKeown, Kiuhara, & Harris, 2012).

The Writer's Workshop, discussed in chapter 9, holds great promise for teaching struggling students. The model accelerates learning through collaborative efforts, the sharing of ideas, a focus on audience and purpose, and measurements of student growth (Crinon, 2012). Collaborative writing occurs when there is no competition among students, but, rather, expectations support common goals along with a sense of shared responsibility and equal accountability (Mercer & Howe, 2012). In addition to supporting writing growth, the writing workshop model supports the development of social skills and social responsibility.

The extensive developments in technology used in classrooms have shifted the way teachers can educate struggling students. Chapter 10, therefore, offers a look into technology and how it can support these students. The incorporation of online tutorials, forums, speech-to-text programs, and word-processing all function to help map, organize, and generate information for the struggling writer.

As students are often more proficient at using technology than teachers, chapter 10 examines how the struggling writer would feel empowered in a more digitalized learning environment. Recent data reveals nearly three in four students in the United States are writing below proficient levels (National Center for Education Statistics, 2012), so embracing new technologies to support and encourage student writing would be critically beneficial.

In totality, this book offers the reader a comprehensive examination of the writing process and describes the necessity of careful teaching to ensure success for all students. It is important to understand evidence-based practices and writing strategies as well as the components needed to produce a well-written and comprehensive body of work. Professional development ensures a deep understanding of writing from the educators' perspective that ensures student outcomes. The authors hope that all who read this tome will find future success in teaching the writing process to students of all ages and abilities.

Acknowledgments

We wish to acknowledge those who made this book possible. We want to thank Elizabeth Jean for her considerable editorial suggestions and manuscript assistance. Your support and input in finalizing this tome were invaluable and very much appreciated. We also wish to acknowledge Melanie Kornacki, our friend and literacy coach from the Springfield Public Schools in Springfield, Massachusetts, for her willingness to write the foreword to this book. Her knowledge of classroom practice and professional development opportunities is impressive, and we appreciated her contributions. Sue Clark also gave willingly of her time to review our manuscript, which clearly made the final document better. Thank you, Sue, for your expertise. Additionally, we wish to recognize Fran Fahey for her editorial input and recommendations. Collectively, this group of professionals made the book stronger, and we are grateful to them all.

Without the gentle push of a good colleague, two authors of this book may have never met. Dr. Richard Holzman of Chester, Massachusetts (who is the senior advisor for external affairs at the University of Massachusetts Amherst and a former graduate dean at American International College where he worked with Nick Young) happened to be a longtime friend of John and Marilyn Alberti of Jacksonville, Florida (who are the uncle and aunt of Bryan Thors Noonan). As the story goes, Richard and John were members of the US Army ROTC Corps of Cadets together fifty-odd years ago at Hofstra University, where they became lifelong friends (and where Richard introduced John to his wife, Marilyn). John and Richard were responsible for hatching the plan to introduce two like-minded writers, Nick and Bryan, and thus the seeds of this book were planted. Kristen then joined the team, and away the three went to complete this tome.

Chapter 1

Defining Evidence Based Practices: Educational Interventions for Struggling Students

Federal legislation such as the Individuals with Disabilities Education Improvement Act of 2004 (IDEIA) as well as the Every Student Succeeds Act (ESSA) of 2015 places an emphasis on improved student outcomes. Critical components of both acts accentuate the use of research-based or evidence-based instructional practices. Evidence-based practices are instructional strategies that have been proven effective through extensive, methodologically sound research studies and include positive outcomes for student achievement over multiple studies (Cook & Cook, 2013; Graham, Harris, & Chambers, 2016).

The setting of high academic standards and pressure to improve student outcomes, combined with a wide range of student ability levels within an inclusive classroom setting, makes the implementation of evidence-based instructional practices not only necessary but required (Samuels, 2016). However, the amount of evidence-based practices identified to benefit students with disabilities is insufficient to address the vast instructional needs of this population (Cook & Smith, 2012; Council for Exceptional Children's Interdivisional Research Group, 2014).

The terms *evidence-based*, *research-based*, and *scientifically based* are used interchangeably and, by definition, incorporate a combination of professional expertise along with supportive empirical research (Great Schools Partnership, 2016; What Works Clearinghouse, 2017). The identification and implementation of evidence-based educational practices work to close the achievement gap by optimizing student outcomes for students with learning disabilities, as well as at-risk students (Cook, Smith, & Tankersley, 2012; Scheeler, Budin, and Markelz, 2016).

The Council for Exceptional Children (CEC) as well as The Institute of Education Sciences (What Works Clearinghouse [WWC]) released

1

standards for identifying evidence-based practices in 2014 and 2015. The CEC evidence-based standards consist of four classifications, as well as eight quality indicators. The WWC evidence-based measures for single-subject research designs consist of six levels of criteria.

An innate exploration into the standards for identifying evidence-based practices is discussed in the following pages. Further, the need to expose teachers to evidence-based practices within teacher preparation programs and throughout the profession is considered and clearly establishes the benefits of such exposure. Finally, the identification and use of high-quality instructional practices are examined and provide additional instructional means for promoting positive student outcomes.

EVIDENCE-BASED INSTRUCTIONAL PRACTICES

Determination of Evidence-Based Educational Practices

To be considered an evidence-based practice, an intervention or strategy must be supported by strong evidence and credible research. The research must demonstrate that the intervention or practice results in positive student outcomes (Cook & Cook, 2013; Graham et al., 2016). Outcomes from evidence-based practices must be specific to a learning area, such as reading comprehension or written expression, and student population, for example, specific learning disability, English language learners, or at-risk students (Council for Exceptional Children, 2014).

For an intervention to have strong evidence to support its effectiveness, there are several conditions that must be met. First, studies must be well designed and consist of randomized controlled trials, comparison-group studies, or single-subject research studies (Duke University, 2017). A randomized controlled trial is a study that randomly selects its participants, has a control group, and measures the effectiveness of the intervention. A comparison-group study compares the outcomes of an intervention between two or more groups of similar demographics and characteristics (Duke University, 2017). A single-subject design study, on the other hand, involves the participant, usually one individual or a small group of individuals, being both the control and treatment group (CEC, 2014; Siegle, 2015).

Second, the quality of the evidence must be strong. Quality of the evidence refers to how meritoriously the study was carried out (CEC, 2014; Siegle, 2015). The experiment should identify every aspect of the study, including such things as who implemented the study, who participated in the study, how the intervention differed from the control group, and a discussion of how the outcomes will affect future research. Further, the results of a study must have reliability and validity to ensure accurate outcomes. Data collection that occurs long term provides the most powerful evidence (CEC, 2014; Siegle, 2015).

THE COUNCIL FOR EXCEPTIONAL CHILDREN EVIDENCE-BASED PRACTICE STANDARDS

The CEC released evidence-based practice standards consisting of quality indicators that define the criteria for evidence-based practices (CEC, 2014). The development of these evidence-based practice standards consisted of several researchers in the field of special education. The workgroup built off the original workings of several research groups (Gersten et al., 2005; Horner, Carr, Halle, McGee, Odom, & Wolery, 2005) that established guidelines for evidence-based practices.

The set of standards developed by the CEC work group are different from previous versions in that they provide separate detailed classifications of evidence-based practices (CEC, 2014). These instructional classifications include evidence-based practices; potentially evidence-based practices; having mixed effects; having negative effects; and having insufficient evidence to categorize their effectiveness (CEC Standards, 2014). Before examining the classifications of evidence-based practices under the CEC standards, an overview of the quality indicators is needed.

CEC has identified eight quality indicators that must be met for an instructional practice to be considered an evidence-based practice. These quality indicators touch on each dimension of a research-based practice and include: context and setting, participants, intervention agent, description of practice, implementation fidelity, internal validity, outcome measures and dependent variables, and data analysis (Browder, Wood, Thompson, & Ribuffo, 2014; CEC, 2014; Cook et al., 2015; Harn, Parisi, & Stoolmiller, 2013).

The context and setting quality indicator assures that sufficient information is provided in the form of descriptive critical features. Some examples of critical features include school demographics, classroom demographics, and curriculum identification. The participants' quality indicator guarantees that the study has thoroughly described the participants, including student demographics, in addition to disabilities or at-risk categories of the participants and the methods used to determine the disability or at-risk status (Browder et al., 2014; CEC, 2014).

The intervention agent quality indicator verifies that the study discusses the role of the researcher (agent), the background variables, and the qualifications and/or training that the agent held or participated in (CEC, 2014; Cook et al., 2015). The description of practice quality indicator ensures a methodical explanation of the intervention procedure, and the agent's actions during the intervention are also provided (CEC, 2014).

Implementation fidelity confirms that the study was conducted with fidelity. To achieve this quality indicator, the study must indicate how fidelity was secured through reliable measurements and implementation strategies (CEC, 2014; Harn, Parisi, and Stoolmiller, 2013). The internal validity quality indicator guarantees that the independent variable was under the control of the researcher, and the study clearly describes the control or comparison group for comparison studies and/or baseline data for single-subject studies.

The study should describe the conditions, curriculum, instruction, and interventions used. The outcome measures and dependent variables quality indicator asserts that the outcomes of the study are linked directly to academic improvement for students. In addition, the study must clearly describe the dependent variables. Finally, the data analysis quality indicator assures that the data analysis techniques employed were appropriate for the type of study and that the study reports an appropriate effect size (Browder et al., 2014; CEC Standards, 2014).

The evidence-based practice standards put forth by the CEC allow for the distinction of five evidence-based classifications to include: evidence-based practice, potentially evidence-based practice, mixed-evidence, insufficient evidence, and negative effects (Browder et al., 2014; Cook et al., 2015). A closer examination into the classifications reveals strict guidelines for each classification label. To be classified as an evidence-based practice, an intervention or strategy must be supported by two or more methodologically sound comparison studies demonstrating positive effects, each with at least sixty participants (Cook et al., 2015).

A potentially evidence-based practice is supported by one to three methodologically sound comparison studies or two to four methodologically sound single-subject studies. A mixed-evidence classification demonstrates that an intervention or strategy has a ratio of no less than 2:1 of methodologically sound studies with positive effects to neutral or mixed effects. A classification of insufficient evidence lacks sufficient research to meet any classification criteria, and a classification of negative effects refers to methodologically sound studies that yield negative effects or the negative effects out weigh any positive effects (CEC Standards, 2014).

THE INSTITUTE OF EDUCATION SCIENCES (WHAT WORKS CLEARINGHOUSE) EVIDENCE-BASED SINGLE-SUBJECT RESEARCH CRITERIA

What Works Clearinghouse, under the umbrella of The Institute of Education Sciences, established review criteria to rate the effectiveness of interventions using single-subject research designs. There are six identification measures:

positive effects, potentially positive effects, mixed effects, potentially negative effects, negative effects, and no discernible effects (Kratochwill et al., 2013; What Works Clearinghouse, 2015). Examination of each identification level reveals the conditions that must be met in order to obtain that classification.

First, specific thresholds are required to be met prior to a team reviewing an intervention. The thresholds include a minimum of five single-case studies examining the intervention, that the single-case studies must be conducted by at least three different research teams, and that the combined number of cases must total at least twenty. The combined number of cases refers to participants, classrooms, schools, and so on. Once these criteria have been met, a review of the studies can occur (Horner, Swaminathan, Sugai, & Smolkowski, 2012; Kratochwill et al., 2013; What Works Clearinghouse, 2015).

The positive effects rating means that 80 percent or more of the single-subject studies produced positive results and no study indicated negative effects, whereas the potentially positive effects rating means that 51–79 percent of the studies produced positive results and no experiment produced negative effects. Moving down the spectrum, the mixed effects rating indicates that at least one study produces positive effects and at least one study results in negative effects or at least one study shows positive effects while at least 50 percent of the studies indicate indeterminate results (What Works Clearinghouse, 2015).

The thresholds continue to deteriorate with the potentially negative effects rating that indicates that 51–79 percent of the studies resulted in negative outcomes and no study showed positive outcomes. Finally, the no-discernible-effects rating indicates that none of the studies resulted in positive or negative effects (What Works Clearinghouse, 2015). The variations in thresholds ensure all studies are viewed the same way and held to the same standards.

A set of questions exist that are meant to assist practitioners when attempting to identify evidence-based practices (Cook et al., 2015; Mather & Wendling, 2012). The first question seeks to identify the quality and strength of the research to support the use of the program or intervention (Horner et al., 2012; Kratochwill et al., 2013). The second question looks to recognize the size of the student population the program or approach will benefit while additionally striving to pinpoint the range of resources included with the program or approach (Mather & Wendling, 2012). Together these questions direct the practitioner to be methodical and careful when looking at and investing in research-based, high-quality interventions.

HIGH-QUALITY INSTRUCTIONAL PRACTICES

Just because a practice is not identified as an evidence-based practice does not mean that the strategy is ineffective (Cook & Cook, 2013; Cook & Odom,

2013). There are several reasons why a useful practice may not be labeled as evidence-based. First, an evidence-based review has not been conducted yet or a review was conducted yet there was a lack of experimental evidence at that point in time (The Council for Exceptional Children's Interdivisional Research Group, 2014).

The lack of identified research-based practices suggests that special education professionals must utilize similar principles for recognizing promising instructional practices supported by available evidence (Puddy & Wilkins, 2011). The idea of high-quality instructional practices insists that the engagement level of students with the instruction provided is the best indicator of quality instruction (Sornson, 2015).

The authors (Mather & Wendling, 2012) discuss three components needed for superior instruction. The first, time on task, refers to the amount of time students spend actively engaged in learning. The second, level of student success, relates to the amount of growth or achievement that occurs throughout the learning process. Finally, the third variable, covered content, relates to the information presented and its relationship to students' lives and interests.

Research suggests that there are nine high-quality instructional practices that have been proven effective with a wide range of learners. These instructional practices include identifying similarities and differences, summarizing and note-taking, reinforcing effort and providing recognition, providing appropriate practice and homework, creating mental or physical images, engagement in cooperative learning opportunities, setting goals and providing feedback, generating and testing hypotheses, and activities that activate prior knowledge (Sornson, 2015).

It is important to note that these high-quality instructional practices engage students in active participation, which is one of the most effective evidence-based teaching practices (Ellis, Worthington, and Larkin, 1994). Prior to Marzano et al., a list of effective teaching practices was developed by Ellis, Worthington, and Larkin (1994). This list included such strategies as active engagement, built-in student success, opportunities for learning, the use of direct instruction, and the implementation of scaffolding instruction. These were used as a jumping-off point for Marzano et al. (2001).

In addition to the previous list, Ellis, Worthington, and Larkin (1994) also included addressing all critical forms of knowledge, organizing and activating knowledge, strategic teaching strategies, explicit instruction, and teaching how things are alike by linking newly learned information to previously learned information as important high-quality teaching strategies. Current research continues to support and prove the effectiveness of these strategies identified by Ellis et al. and Marzano et al. (Sheeler et al., 2016; Sornson, 2015).

THE NEED FOR EXPOSURE TO EVIDENCE-BASED PRACTICES IN PROFESSIONAL DEVELOPMENT

Research, along with federal mandates, supports the need for teacher preparation programs to expose teacher candidates (both general education and special education) to educational evidence-based practices. Both federal and state mandates, most notably the Individuals with Disabilities Education Improvement Act, 2004 (IDEIA), clearly state that teachers need to be trained in how to identify and implement evidence-based practices (Browder et al., 2014).

Teacher candidates should be exposed to the use of evidence-based special education practices through both theory and practice, resulting in well-informed practitioners once out in the field. Preparation programs must ensure that teacher candidates can select appropriate interventions and practices that are supported by empirical research and be able to implement the practice with fidelity (Browder et al., 2014; Scheeler et al., 2016; Sornson, 2015).

Teachers who are well prepared, including with exposure to the use of evidence-based practices, are more likely to remain in the field, thus creating stable educational environments that promote positive student outcomes. Finally, increasing evidence proves that evidence-based practices implemented consistently and with fidelity improves student outcomes (Kretlow & Helf, 2013). A closer examination of providing exposure to evidence-based practices through a variety of professional development opportunities will be discussed in a later chapter.

FINAL THOUGHTS

Federal mandates have required the reliable and consistent use of evidence-based or scientific-based instructional practices within all K–12 public school settings. The consistent use of evidence-based practices has proven beneficial for a wide range of students including those with disabilities and those considered at-risk (Cook et al., 2012; Graham et al., 2016; Scheeler et al., 2016). To be considered an evidence-based instructional practice, the approach must be supported by quality research that demonstrates positive student outcomes (Browder et al., 2015; Graham, Harris, & Chambers, 2016).

In 2014 the Council for Exceptional Children (CEC) identified eight quality indicators for identifying the effectiveness of evidence-based practices. The quality indicators assist review teams in identifying the appropriate classification of the evidence-based practice as well. CEC additionally developed five categories of classifications that review study validity (Browder et al., 2014; CEC Standards, 2014). In addition to CEC, the Institute of Education Sciences categorized criteria for reviewing interventions conducted using single-subject design studies similar to those of CEC (What Works Clearing-house, 2015).

Cook and Cook (2013) and Cook and Odom (2013) remind us that a strategy may still be effective regardless if it has been identified as evidence-based. There are two reasons why a strategy may not be listed as evidence-based, including not having sufficient experimental research or not having an evidence-based review conducted (Council for Exceptional Children's Interdivisional Research Group, 2014).

POINTS TO REMEMBER

- *Federal mandates require the consistent use of evidence-based instructional practices.*
- *The identification and implementation of evidence-based educational practices work to close the achievement gap by optimizing student outcomes.*
- *To be considered an evidence-based practice, an intervention or strategy must be supported by strong evidence and credible research.*
- *There are limited identified evidence-based practices for students with disabilities and some strategies work that have yet to be identified as research-based.*

Chapter 2

Applying Evidence-Based Practices to Writing Instruction: A Review of Effective Programs

With the adoption of the Common Core State Standards (2017), proficiency in written expression has taken a giant leap forward. Writing skills are critical to pass high-stakes testing as well as a requirement for graduation (Flanagan & Bouck, 2015). In addition, at the postsecondary level, writing samples are used to evaluate a student's qualifications for acceptance (Troia & Olinghouse, 2013). According to the National Center for Education Statistics (2012), it is estimated that only 27 percent of students in grades 8 and 12 are proficient or higher in writing, and an alarming 74 percent are below the proficiency level (Harris & Graham, 2013).

The process of writing involves a combination of cognitive, linguistic, affective, and behavioral means (Troia & Olinghouse, 2013). For students with learning disabilities (LD) or for students who struggle with writing, the process can be frustrating and overwhelming, resulting in a lack of motivation to write. The use of evidence-based instructional practices in teaching writing offers effective strategies for teaching writing skills while developing motivational and self-regulation proficiencies for students who struggle.

Graham et al. (2016) discuss the influence of using evidence-based practices as a means of professional and student growth. The authors suggest that an understanding of evidence-based practices plays a huge role in supporting the conscious decision of choosing what is best for each individual student based upon his or her abilities as well as weaknesses. Evidence-based teaching strategies are instructional practices that have been identified, through extensive research, to promote academic growth or remediate weaknesses (Graham, Harris, & Chambers, 2016).

Specific learning disabilities can affect areas of written expression, including spelling accuracy, grammar and punctuation, handwriting, and organization and clarity of written expression (Connelly & Dockrell, 2016).

9

These same areas of weakness can also be prevalent in struggling students. Despite these deficits, there are several evidence-based strategies, such as Self-Regulated Strategy Development, Writer's Workshop, and a few writing programs, which have been shown to be effective for students with learning disabilities, as well as students who simply struggle with writing.

EDUCATIONAL LEGISLATION AND COMMON CORE STATE STANDARDS

Educational Legislation

Educational legislation, including the Individuals with Disabilities Education Improvement Act of 2004 (IDEIA) and the Every Student Succeeds Act (ESSA) (2015), specifically require the use of evidence-based or research-based instructional practices. The use of scientifically backed teaching practices is an attempt to provide the absolute best instructional strategies to close the achievement gap.

The ESSA was passed into law in December 2015. The law replaces the No Child Left Behind Act, which had previously replaced the long-standing Elementary and Secondary Education Act (ESEA). The goals of ESSA are to expand educational opportunities and improve student outcomes. These goals will be accomplished through equal opportunity to quality instruction and accountability (U.S. Department of Education, n.d.).

A few critical aspects of ESSA include the funding for literacy programs focused on evidence-based literacy instruction, including writing instruction, the incorporation of Universal Design for Learning Principles, and state-set goals for struggling students (Lee, n.d.). The federally funded literacy programs under ESSA (U.S. Department of Education, 2015) include a national center for literacy and literacy education grants, which allow schools' access to evidence-based tools for teaching literacy components, including writing (Lee, n.d.; U.S. Department of Education, n.d.).

Under IDEIA, the implementation of research-based interventions are required to be used within the Response to Intervention (RTI) framework as a means to identify the presence of specific learning disabilities instead of the discrepancy model which may not be as accurate (Wright, 2004; Troia, 2013). In the case of RTI, it is assumed that evidence-based interventions and strategies are implemented at each tier, including tier 1 in the general education classroom; however, there is a lack of consistent implementation across states and school districts.

The instruction of writing is one of the most complex areas of teaching for a couple of reasons (Troia, 2013). In relation to an RTI framework, Troia supports these assumptions on writing assessment and extensive research. First, there is a lack of coherent writing assessment methods. Assessing writing is difficult and may be inconsistent between evaluators. Second, much research geared toward RTI interventions has been solely focused on reading improvement due to federal initiatives such as Reading First (Troia, 2013).

Common Core State Standards

The Common Core State Standards place an extensive emphasis on written expression (Troia & Olinghouse, 2013). As a result, the importance of teaching writing is at a critical point within the educational system. However, research suggests that there are impediments to implementing evidence-based writing practices.

Hindrances such as lack of teacher training in writing instruction, inadequate professional development around how to teach writing, and a lack of coherent curricular materials for addressing the emphasis on written expression all contribute to the absence of consistent and effective writing instruction (Gilbert & Graham, 2010; Troia & Olinghouse, 2013). In order to ensure quality writing instruction for all students, across all grade levels and content areas, more research is needed to understand and identify efficacious evidence-based writing strategies.

Defining the Disability and the Struggle

Students who struggle with writing may display similar characteristics as students labeled as having a learning disability. In addition, students who struggle with writing may present with any of the following characteristics: difficulty producing and organizing ideas, lack of vocabulary to sufficiently express their ideas, frequent frustration, and avoidance of written assignments (Adkins, 2013; Culham, 2011).

According to the IDEIA, a specific learning disability "means a disorder in one or more of the basic psychological processes involved in understanding or in using language, spoken or written, that may manifest itself in the imperfect ability to listen, think, speak, read, write, spell, or to do mathematical calculations, including conditions such as perceptual disabilities, brain injuries, minimal brain function, dyslexia, and development aphasia" (2004).

Three specific disorders fall under the broad category of learning disabilities that specifically relate to discrepancies in written expression including dyslexia, language learning disorder, and development coordination disorder (Connelly & Dockrell, 2016). An examination of the three offers distinct characteristics and differences in their hindrance of writing development and writing success. Dyslexia is characterized by an extreme difficulty in learning to read and spell specifically with rapid letter naming and phonological aspects of reading and spelling, which present difficulties in written expression (Connelly & Dockrell, 2016; Shaywitz, 2003).

Language Learning Disorder (LLD), also referred to as a language-based learning disability or specific language impairment, directly affects the development and processing of oral language as well as the structure of the language system (Harris & Graham, 2013). Individuals with LLD may experience difficulty in expressing ideas orally or in written form, vocabulary development, comprehending questions presented orally or visually, identifying letter sounds, spelling words correctly, and understanding left to right progression (Stone, Silliman, Ehren, & Wallach, 2014).

Extensive complexities encompassing this disorder cause individuals to struggle greatly in learning to read as well as producing written language. Individuals with LLD experience clear difficulties throughout school, especially in the areas mentioned (Dockrell, Lindsay, & Connelly, 2009). With regard to written expression, the authors reveal that the writing pieces produced by students with LLD are usually short and display numerous errors in spelling, flow, and clarity (Harris & Graham, 2013).

Development coordination disorder (DCD) directly affects the use of coordinated motor skills, as well as performing and learning movement tasks, such as handwriting (Harris & Graham, 2013). When students have difficulty with handwriting, the writing process, including written expression, is jeopardized. Students with DCD display a struggle with handwriting, often writing at a much slower rate and produce far less work than typical peers (Connelly & Dockrell, 2016).

How the Writing Process Is Affected When Students Struggle

Research suggests that the most prevalent characteristics of writing weaknesses for students who struggle or who have learning disabilities pertain to spelling inaccuracies and deficits in writing fluency (Beringer, Lee, Abbott, & Breznitz, 2013; Harris & Graham, 2013). There is a direct link between reading and spelling difficulties and written expression (Connelly & Dockrell, 2016). If students struggle to master the foundational skills involved in learning to read, such as understanding phonemic awareness, the alphabetic principle, and spelling, the results are poor for writing development (Connelly & Dockrell, 2016).

During the writing process, struggling students, or those with learning disabilities, may experience difficulties with components such as planning what to write, goal-setting, organizing their thoughts, expressing ideas, and revising what they have written (Harris & Graham, 2013). The writing process integrates a complex set of skills, which can be affected by impairments in short- and long-term working memory, as evidenced in students with dyslexia (Beringer et al., 2013). These impairments directly affect the ability to successfully execute multiple cognitive tasks.

Self-Regulated Strategy Development Approach

Self-regulated strategy development (SRSD) is an evidence-based approach used to assist in developing both the writing skills and motivation of students with writing difficulties. Meta-analyses have proven that SRSD has "the strongest impact of any strategies instruction approach in writing and is among the strongest currently researched interventions for writing" (Harris & Graham, 2013, p. 74).

SRSD has also been found to be very effective for students with attention deficit hyperactivity disorder (ADHD). Students with ADHD, like students with LD, experience deficits with executive functioning and working memory (Taft & Mason, 2011). SRSD combines explicit instruction with opportunities for supported independent practice. Explicit instruction in goal-setting, self-monitoring, self-instruction, and self-reinforcement are prevalent in the SRSD approach (Ennis, Jolivette, Terry, Frederick, & Alberto, 2015).

There are six stages for implementation of the SRSD approach. These stages include building background knowledge, teacher discussion of the strategies involved, teacher modeling of the strategies, student memorization of the strategies, teacher support during the writing process and use of the strategies, and independent practice (De La Paz & Sherman, 2013; Ennis et al., 2015; Johnson, Hancock, Carter, & Pool, 2012).

When building background knowledge, teachers need to understand the unique writing abilities and provide appropriate foundational knowledge as needed. Once background knowledge has been discussed, the teacher must discuss the purpose of the writing strategies that will be taught (Harris & Graham, 2013). Discussions should begin with the identification of what it is that good writers do, should occur between teacher and students, as well as peer to peer, and should be focused around the strategies identified as good writing.

Discussions should also incorporate visuals such as charts or graphic organizers in order to support strategy development and memory throughout the process. After discussions have occurred, the teacher should model how to utilize the specific strategy. Modeling the writing process out loud, similar to a "read aloud, think aloud," allows the students to comprehend the thought process behind the strategy (Harris & Graham, 2013). The next period, memorization, involves student practice using the strategy or strategies learned.

Practice should be supported through partner, group, and individual opportunities, as well as utilization of mnemonic devices. Once students have memorized the strategies, teachers should provide scaffolded support throughout the writing process. Guided support includes such practices as collaborative writing, the use of prompting, as well as self-monitoring strategies. Finally, independent practice is achieved when students can independently use the strategies, including self-monitoring and goal-setting (Harris & Graham, 2013).

Self-Regulation Strategy Development Using Mnemonic Devices

The SRSD approach has several mnemonic devices that support students through the writing process (Del La Paz & Sherman, 2013; Harris & Graham, 2013; Johnson et al., 2012). Mnemonic devices such as POW, PLAN, TREE, STOP, DARE, FIX, and WWW are powerful support strategies that support students in identifying the steps necessary to accomplish the writing task at hand and prompting a response.

The POW strategy stands for *pick my idea, organize my notes, write and say more.* This strategy assists students with brainstorming ideas, outlining ideas and notes, as well as adding details to what they write. The PLAN strategy is geared toward more complex writing tasks such as informational pieces.

PLAN refers to *pay attention to the prompt, list the main ideas to develop your essay, add supporting details, and number the major points* (Harris, Graham, MacArthur, Reid, & Mason, 2011). The TREE mnemonic stands for *topic sentence, reasons, ending, and examine.* Both the TREE and POW mnemonics can be combined to assist with persuasive writing tasks.

The STOP and DARE mnemonics are often used together for persuasive essays as well. STOP refers to *suspend judgment, take a side, organize ideas, and plan more as you write.* The DARE strategy signifies *develop your topic sentence, add supporting ideas, reject at least one argument for the other side, and end with a conclusion* (Ennis et al., 2015).

The last two mnemonic devices, FIX and WWW, represent *focus on essay elements, identify problems, and execute changes* and *who, when, and where.* The FIX strategy is useful for guiding students when revising their work. The WWW strategy works well with story writing tasks (De La Paz & Sherman, 2013; Johnson et al., 2012).

Accommodations and Instructional Approaches to Assist Struggling Writers

Several pundits (Connelly & Dockrell, 2016; Morin, 2014; Troia, 2013) identify a variety of instructional accommodations and approaches that benefit students with LD or those that struggle with writing. Through the use of classroom accommodations and instructional practices, students who struggle with writing can feel supported which in turn can increase motivation for writing. Some of the accommodations and approaches shown to be effective include:

- Providing extra time to complete written assignments
- Decreasing the amount and/or complexity of writing assignments
- Using graphic organizers
- Grading based on written concepts and not handwriting or spelling
- Providing examples of finished work
- Breaking writing tasks into smaller chunks
- Teaching and implementing the use of rubrics

Extensive research studies (Troia, 2013; Troia & Olinghouse, 2013) have identified critical components needed to provide effective writing programs for struggling writers. Components such as the following create writing programs that meet the wide range of academic levels and individual needs.

- Setting clear, specific, and attainable writing goals for struggling writers
- Explicitly teaching aspects of writing composition, constructing paragraphs, revising and editing, as well as sentence construction
- Providing encouragement and teaching self-monitoring skills
- Providing opportunities for students to collaborate in the drafting, planning, and revising processes
- Dedicating time for writing across curricular areas
- Modeling, explaining, and scaffolding instructions
- Setting high expectations
- Implementing the use of portfolios and assigning grades reflecting growth over time

Writer's Workshop

Writer's Workshop is a well-established instructional model that focuses on the writing process instead of simply producing written products (Kissel & Miller, 2015; Troia, 2013). Significant components included in this model include providing a predictable routine, teacher modeling of skills, strategies and the writing process, peer-to-peer as well as teacher-to-student conferences, setting high expectations, scaffolding instruction with frequent feedback, cooperative learning environments, and opportunities for self-regulation provide the foundation for a successful Writer's Workshop model (Kissel & Miller, 2015; Troia, 2013).

Fu and Shelton (2007) conducted a study focusing on the effects of a Writer's Workshop model on students with LD within an inclusion classroom. The study included twenty-nine students, and nine of them were identified as having a disability affecting learning. Shelton, a fourth-grade classroom teacher, was looking for a more inclusive way to teach her students with disabilities.

Prior to entering Shelton's classroom, students with LD were taught to write in a "linear, step-by-step process: brainstorm on a specific planning worksheet in response to a prompt provided by the teacher, transfer the planned writing to a narrative or essay frame, edit and make corrections, submit the work to the teacher, and recopy the teacher's corrections as the final copy" (Fu & Shelton, 2007, p. 326). Shelton utilized the Writer's Workshop model within her fourth-grade classroom.

Students were expected to create their own topics for writing, set appropriate and attainable goals, confer with their peers and the teacher throughout the process, and share their work publicly once completed. The writer's workshop followed a fifty-minute routine including a minilesson or read-aloud at the beginning before students started their independent writing. The minilessons focused on a specific strategy or brainstorming activity. A read-aloud allowed the students to connect ideas to their own lives as a basis for writing (Fu & Shelton, 2007).

After the minilesson or read-aloud, students were free to write independently or collaborate with a peer or small group. Throughout the independent writing time, the teacher would conference with students in order to provide scaffolded support, feedback, and encouragement. The idea behind the Writer's Workshop is to encourage peer collaboration as well as supporting peer-to-peer discourse, through the sharing of ideas, supporting one another through the writing process, and respecting each other as a valued member of the classroom community (Fu & Shelton, 2007).

As a result of this study, all nine students identified as having a learning disability made substantial gains in the area of written expression, as well as social gains. Through the use of a Writer's Workshop model there is an emphasis placed upon not only the writing process but on also community building. The concept of self-selected partners and groups, as well as publicly sharing finished products, supports the idea of classroom communities (Fu & Shelton, 2007). Behymer (2003) discusses the impact of Writer's Workshop in a kindergarten classroom.

Although there are similarities between the Writer's Workshop routine mentioned previously, at the kindergarten level the writing focus may be different. For instance, minilessons spotlight phonics, spelling, spacing of words, punctuation, and simple sentences. A huge part of the kindergarten Writer's Workshop is known as interactive writing, which provides critical modeling opportunities that help young children make progress in their own writing (Behymer, 2003; Fountas & Pinnell, 2001; McCarrier, Fountas, & Pinnell, 2000).

The kindergarten Writer's Workshop consists of six steps lasting approximately thirty to forty minutes. The first, known as the drawing stage, incorporates drawings and symbols as prewriting organizers. The second step, referred to as kid-writing, emphasizes guided phonics-based spelling. Children are taught to listen to the sounds they hear in words and write the corresponding letters down. If they cannot identify the corresponding letter for the sound they hear, a magic line is used to represent the unidentified sound (Behymer, 2003).

The third step incorporates adult underwriting and individual minilessons. This is where the teacher reads the words or symbols that the student has written and writes the correct conventional spelling of the word(s) at the bottom of the page. This time also allows for individual minilessons that can be tailored to individual student needs. The fourth step includes a whole group minilesson.

During this time, a few students are encouraged to share their stories in the author's chair, while their peers ask questions or make connections. The fifth step encompasses mini-sharing. Students are supported in sharing their stories with peers during partner time. Finally, the sixth step, known as the publication stage, focuses on revision and editing. Published work is then displayed in a classroom book or bulletin board (Behymer, 2003).

Some similarities between the kindergarten and upper elementary Writer's Workshops include the opportunities to choose partners or groups to work with, the incorporation of minilessons, the sharing of written products, as well as guided support and encouragement. Differences include specialty paper at the youngest levels, the incorporation of drawing, and the use of markers for younger writers with smaller hands. Markers can be a motivator; they are brightly colored and easy to work with. The tips do not break, so students must cross out their mistakes allowing the educator to visualize the thought process that went into the work (Behymer, 2003).

Lucy Calkins's *Up the Ladder* Writing Curriculum

The Lucy Calkins's curriculum *Up the Ladder* writing program by Heinemann provides resources focused on effective instruction, principles, methods, and structure for the Writer's Workshop model. The *Up the Ladder* writing curriculum was designed, after much research, by the dedicated colleagues at the Teachers College Reading and Writing Project (TCRWP). Individuals within the TCRWP invested significant time in researching the instructional ingredients necessary for accelerating growth in narrative, informative, and opinion writing for students across all grade levels and all ability levels (Calkins, n.d.).

Within the various writing units, students practice small writing samples specific to a certain genre. Students are supported throughout the phases of the writing process including planning, drafting, and revising. One unique aspect of the program is the incorporation of hands-on learning. Each lesson booklet has students cut pages apart to make concrete manipulative revisions to their writing (Calkins, n.d.; Heinemann, n.d.). In addition, teachers are provided with tremendous support in the form of downloadable online resources; links to digital texts; and samples of student work, videos, and checklists.

Being a Writer Writing Curriculum

The *Being a Writer* writing curriculum was developed incorporating the extensive research of Richard Allington, Donald Graves, and the National Council of Teachers of English on writing, motivation, and learning. As a result, the *Being a Writer* curriculum focuses on social interaction, collaborative learning opportunities, teacher modeling, teacher and peer conferencing, daily writing practice, self-assessment strategies, and writing for real audiences (Center for the Collaborative Classroom, 2017).

Being a Writer curriculum combines both academic and social emotional learning and was inspired by the Writer's Workshop model. The curriculum focuses on two goals: developing the creativity and skills of a writer and developing the social and ethical values of a responsible individual. Instruction in all stages of the writing cycle is addressed, including drafting, revising, proofreading, and publishing. Teachers are provided with both print and digital resources, including curriculum-based assessments (Center for the Collaborative Classroom, 2017).

Development of social and ethical responsibility is supported through structured cooperative partner work, pair conferencing, discussing and solving problems, as well as enhanced discussions through teacher prompting. As a result, students learn how to show respect, fairness, inclusion, and responsibility (Center for the Collaborative Classroom, 2017).

The Vermont Writing Collaborative

The Vermont Writing Collaborative is a nonprofit organization comprised of public school teachers dedicated to providing writing development for all students. The collaborative offers a writing curriculum referred to as *Writing for Understanding*. This approach asserts that students must first deeply understand a topic they are writing about if they are going to be successful in the writing process. *Writing for Understanding* combines three strategies: backward design, emphasis on understanding, and direct instruction (Vermont Writing Collaborative, 2017a).

Backward design or backward planning, developed in 1998 by Grant Wiggins and Jay McTighe (2005), is an approach to teaching that starts with the end in mind. *Writing for Understanding* identified the big ideas and created content and resources that aid students in learning. The emphasis on understanding focuses on creating meaning through a deep understanding of the task or topic being addressed. This is created and supported through the use of concrete examples and rich texts (Vermont Writing Collaborative, 2017a).

Direct instruction is a staple in any classroom where there are students with exceptionalities and those that struggle. It is the third component of the Writing for *Understanding strategy*. As a proven instructional practice, it requires explicit teaching of content, tasks, or skills followed by scaffolded practice with on-going support (Vermont Writing Collaborative, 2017a).

FINAL THOUGHTS

IDEIA and ESSA both stress the use of evidence-based instructional practices to close the achievement gap across all curricular areas in students who are struggling or who have learning disabilities (Lee, n.d.; Troia, 2013). In addition, the adoption of the Common Core State Standards places heavy emphasis on written expression, thus encouraging the use of evidence-based teaching practices in the area of writing. However, there continue to be hindrances to effective implementation (Troia & Olinghouse, 2013).

The writing process is a complex endeavor that incorporates several cognitive, linguistic, affective, and behavior skills (Troia & Olinghouse, 2013). For students identified as having a specific learning disability, the writing process can prove to be challenging. Deficits in working and long-term memory, as well as executive function, make the writing process difficult and as a result decrease motivation to write (Graham et al., 2016). Students who struggle with writing might experience difficulties with planning, goal-setting, expressing ideas, and revising strategies (Adkins, 2013; Culham, 2011; Harris & Graham, 2013; Mason et al., 2011).

One evidence-based instructional model known as Self-Regulation Development Strategy (SRSD) has been proven to show significant improvement for students with LD (Harris & Graham, 2013). SRSD includes explicit instruction in goal-setting, self-monitoring, self-instruction, as well as self-reinforcement and instruction and guided practice in specific writing strategies, and is presented in six stages (Ennis et al., 2015; De LaPaz & Sherman, 2013; Johnson, Hancock, Carter, & Pool, 2012).

Another promising evidence-based instructional model, Writer's Workshop, focuses on the process of writing while providing teacher and peer support (Troia, 2013). The ideas behind Writer's Workshop support the development of writing skills through the establishment of community, peer support and respect, teacher and peer conferencing, as well as publicly sharing written products. Writer's Workshops have been shown to be effective for students with disabilities, by increasing written expression as well as socialization skills (Behymer, 2003; Fu & Shelton, 2007; Troia, 2013).

Building off the strengths of the Writer's Workshop model, several writing programs have been developed. Programs such as *Up the Ladder*, *Being a Writer*, and *Writing for Understanding* focus on development of writing skills through collaboration and a sense of community. These writing programs offer tremendous support for teachers and were developed through extensive research in effective writing development, social and emotional learning, as well as the needs of struggling writers (Calkins, n.d.; Center for Collaborative Learning, 2017; Vermont Writing Collaborative, 2017a).

POINTS TO REMEMBER

- *Evidence-based instructional practices are mandated under IDEIA and ESSA, as well as incorporated into the Common Core State Standards across curricular domains.*
- *Writing is a complex process involving cognitive, linguistic, affective, and behavioral skills working together.*
- *Students with learning disabilities may experience difficulties in planning, organizing their thoughts, expressing their thoughts, spelling, and revising when writing.*
- *Self-Regulation Strategy Development (SRSD) is a significantly effective evidence-based practice for increasing the writing process for students with LD. SRSD incorporates instruction in goal-setting, self-monitoring, and self-regulation in conjunction with teaching writing strategies.*
- *Writer's Workshop is an evidence-based writing model that incorporates explicit teaching of writing strategies along with peer collaboration, independent choice, conferencing, and community building.*

Chapter 3

High Quality Professional Development: Promising Approaches

Federal and state regulations, including the IDEIA and the ESSA, prescribe the necessary ingredients for successful student achievement, including the use of evidence-based practices and access to resources. These same regulations stress the importance of effective professional development for improving teacher performance and ultimately student achievement (Green & Allen, 2015). Many educational policymakers, as well as educators themselves, understand the importance of worthwhile professional development to promote excellent teaching skills and ultimately raise student achievement (DeMonte, 2013).

Professional development plays a vital role in improving teaching and learning. Meaningful professional development promotes the implementation of successful instructional strategies and, as a result, supports all students in meeting curriculum standards (Marrongelle, Sztajn, & Smith, 2013). Professional development, therefore, should focus on research-based pedagogical strategies in order to support teaching and learning outcomes (Bowe & Gore, 2017).

Many new teachers feel that their preservice education was insufficient to fully prepare them to be effective once stepping into the classroom (Cannon, Swoszowski, Gallagher, & Easterbrooks, 2012). One way to support the continuous growth of new teachers, as well as experienced teachers, is to ensure consistent and meaningful professional development opportunities in conjunction with mentoring and collaborative approaches (Geeraerts et al., 2015).

For professional development to be effective, it must incorporate collaborative approaches, time for reflection, coherence to other professional development opportunities, and be determined by individual needs (Earley & Porritt, 2014; Lauer, Christopher, Firpo-Triplett, & Buchting, 2014). In addition, under federal guidelines, school districts are held accountable for providing valuable professional development for their educators (Green & Allen, 2015).

A correlation exists between high-performing schools and school improvement strategies (including professional development) that focus on supporting the behaviors of educators in the way they deliver effective instruction. School leaders of high-performing schools tend to focus professional development efforts on supporting and increasing high-quality instructional practices within the classrooms (DeMonte, 2013).

PROFESSIONAL DEVELOPMENT

The term *professional development*, within the realm of education, refers to improving teaching and learning through strategies designed to support, change, and/or develop teaching practices (Green & Allen, 2015; Lauer et al., 2014). Successful professional development should be focused on the specific population of the students served and relevant to current instruction (Earley & Porritt, 2014). Unfortunately, meaningful professional development that is focus-driven and meaningful continues to be thin, sporadic, and rare across school districts in the United States (Bowe & Gore, 2017; DeMonte, 2013).

Characteristics of High-Quality Professional Development

Professional development is the link between the goals of educational reforms and the implementation and success of the reforms within schools (Demonte, 2013). The Every Student Succeeds Act of 2015 and previously the No Child Left Behind Act of 2001 both recognize the components of high-quality, research-based professional development that is focused and aligned with curriculum standards and support the school improvement priorities and goals. Additionally, all educator learning opportunities should be intensive and continuous, sustainable within the classroom and school environment, and should build strong collegial relationships (Green & Allen, 2015).

Bubb (2013) developed nine stages of professional development that encompass a continuous cycle of professional growth. Divided into three components, they include: the *domain of preparation*, which embodies four junctures, including identifying needs, obtaining a baseline picture, goal-setting, and creating a plan of how to achieve the goal(s). The second component, *domain of learning*, focuses on two stages: activity development and the occurrence of new learning. The final stage, *domain of improvement,* encompasses three stages including putting learning into practice, an impact on student learning, and improved teacher self-efficacy.

Professional development is important because it can improve the way teachers provide instruction and improve student learning (Krasnoff, 2015). This claim is supported by identifying the key components of any successful professional development opportunity. Components include focus on content and how students learn active learning opportunities and collaborative participation and have sufficient duration. The link between teaching writing through valuable professional development is explored next.

TYPES OF PROFESSIONAL DEVELOPMENT

General Professional Development Opportunities

Professional learning communities. Professional learning communities embrace the idea of learning through collaboration, collegial partnerships, shared values and visions, as well as a shared responsibility for student learning (Bowe & Gore, 2017). Professional learning communities offer an alternative way to conducting professional development. Implementation of quality instructional rounds presents a great opportunity for this to occur (Bowe & Gore, 2017).

Instructional rounds were developed by Richard Elmore (City, Elmore, Fiarman, & Teitel, 2010). Elmore adapted his instructional rounds from medical rounds conducted throughout medical residencies consisting of three phases that linked problems of practice with improvement efforts (Bowe & Gore, 2017). The use of instructional rounds was explicitly "designed to bring discussions of instruction directly into the process of school improvement . . . it creates a common discipline and focus among practitioners with a common purpose and set of problems" (City, Elmore, Fiarman, & Teitel, 2010, p.3).

A close examination of the phases of instructional rounds reveals similarities to the workshop model of instruction that educators often use in their classrooms. The first phase of instructional rounds includes engagement in professional reading and discussion where educators are able to learn about teaching and learning. The second phase involves classroom observations and is critical as educators reflect on lessons and how that relates to their own classroom practice. The third and final phase occurs when educators come back together to engage in conversation while analyzing the observed teaching as a means to improve their own (Bowe & Gore, 2017).

The use of professional learning communities with the implementation of instructional rounds may be useful for improving instruction in writing. For example, if instructional rounds were implemented as described previously, teachers would start by reading an article or chapter pertaining to writing instruction, such as a specific writing strategy. After the reading and initial discussion, teachers would then perform the "rounds" and then reconvene to discuss what they observed in relation to the writing strategy and how this will improve their own practice.

Self-study. It is important for educators to actively engage in research that will improve teaching and learning in the classrooms (Vanassche & Kelchtermans, 2016). Mills (2014) defines action research as "any systematic inquiry conducted by teacher researchers . . . in the teaching/learning environment to gather information about how their schools operate, how they teach, and how well their students learn. The information is gathered with the goals of gaining insight, developing reflective practices, effecting positive change in the school environment, and improving student outcomes" (p. 458).

Action research can be considered a form of self-study. Action research involves an educator identifying an area of concern or focus related to teaching and learning, such as writing. The educator collects and analyzes data related to the chosen focus, interprets the data, and then develops a plan of action (Mills, 2014; Vanassche & Kelchtermans, 2016). Action research can be conducted individually or within a group of educators who may have the same concerns.

The personalized nature of action research means it is beneficial to individual educators. Some of the benefits of conducting action research include meeting individual professional practice needs, identifying and addressing individual student learning needs, and engagement in continuous learning experiences through professional development opportunities (Annenberg Foundation, 2017).

Mentoring and coaching. Mentoring and coaching provides guidance and support and fosters positive experiences. The importance of strong mentoring relationships to reverse the high teacher turnover rates cannot be denied (Marshall et al., 2013). The contributing factors to teachers leaving the profession within the first few years include a lack of emotional support and inadequate resources and materials (Marshall et al., 2013).

Effective professional development should instruct teachers in evidence-based instructional practices proven to support student achievement. Educators who are explicitly taught these instructional practices, through mentorship or coaching partnerships, and where modeling, ongoing support, and feedback are present on a continuous basis, will gain positive outcomes in personal performance and student growth (Desimone & Pak, 2017).

Peer group mentoring is a model developed in Finland for supporting professional development efforts (Geeraerts et al., 2015). This model has proven essential in strengthening teacher efficiency across their teacher careers. Peer group models consist of both new and experienced teachers from various schools within a district. Groups typically have between five and ten participants who are responsible for planning, organizing, and implementing their own agendas for professional development (Geeraerts et al., 2015).

Peer group mentoring and support systems have proven beneficial as educators are exposed to various teaching strategies and different perspectives. Through classroom observation, open discussions, and sharing of ideas, trust is built between educators. Peer mentoring models focus on collaboration and teamwork; thus, once teachers feel comfortable with shared ideas and tools, they can be added to a personal teaching repertoire (Osten & Gidseg, n.d.). Teachers who are open with students about their desire to improve as an educator model skills essential for success (Osten & Gidseg, n.d.).

Partnerships. Collaborative partnerships between school districts and postsecondary institutions play an important role in developing, supporting, and maintaining effective professional development opportunities for educators. The benefits of these partnerships include those to preservice educators but also offer coordinated support throughout their teaching careers (Colwell, MacIsaac, Tichenor, Heins, & Piechura, 2014; Marrongelle et al., 2013).

The National Council for the Accreditation of Teacher Education (NCATE) developed standards for professional development schools. The standards encompass essential characteristics by providing a framework based on a consensus of what a professional development school should include and how to accommodate and develop such schools (Colwell et. al., 2014). The NCATE standards include five focus areas: standard 1: learning community; standard 2: accountability and quality assurance; standard 3: collaboration; standard 4: diversity and equity; and standard 5: structure, resources, and roles.

A qualitative study (Colwell et al., 2014) examined the NCATE standards from the perspective of school principals and their partnerships with local colleges and universities. Four critical themes emerged, including relevance of professional development activities, collaboration and partnership, planned and data-driven professional development activities, and professional development activities that are aligned with what is occurring in the classrooms.

The results of this study (Colwell et al., 2014) indicate that the NCATE standards do play an important role in ensuring the sustainability of professional development partnerships. Specifically, data collected from both school principals and their college partners indicated agreement in the importance in standards 1, 2, and 3 to sustain effective partnerships. Similarly, both groups showed less emphasis placed on standards 4 and 5. Although both groups felt standards 4 and 5 were important, they played less of a role in guaranteeing stability of the partnership (Colwell et. al., 2014).

Writing Specific Professional Development

Vermont Writing Collaborative

Although the Vermont Writing Collaborative has a methodology, Writing for Understanding (Hawkins et al., 2008), the group is also heavily involved in the professional development of educators in order to spread their writing message. With an emphasis on deep understanding and direct instruction, educators are taught to plan with the end in mind, an Understanding by Design key concept (Wiggins & McTighe, 1998).

The website includes hundreds of free documents including student work, content-based writing/reading tasks, videos, research packs, and, most of all, the painted essay. The painted essay is a written and color-coded visual for students—red for the introduction, yellow and blue for the proof paragraphs, and green (a mixture of yellow and blue) for the conclusion (Vermont Writing Collaborative, 2017b). Although some resources are available for free, nothing compares to having the team in the building for professional development.

In addition to the school year professional development opportunities, the Vermont Writing Collaborative offers an intensive summer institute where educators spend an entire week deep in the methodology of Writing for Understanding. The learning includes discussions on the Common Core, focus questions/statement, backward design, close reading, building and working with knowledge, structures and models, and gradual release and assessment (Vermont Writing Collaborative, 2016). Once the institute is over, educators are ready to go do the work of teaching students.

Keys to Literacy. This program is specific and focuses literacy professional development for K–12 educators (Keys to Literacy, n.d.). Founded in 2007, the organization offers educational opportunities "based on sound research, best practice and delivered by expert teacher trainers" (n.p.) in four areas including writing, comprehension, phonics, and vocabulary and at the primary, elementary, middle, and high school levels (Keys to Literacy, n.d.).

Keys to Literacy (KTL) is a sustained professional development program that is implemented schoolwide using peer-coaching, collaboration, and observation. Beginning with the formation of a personalized plan, the team trains the educators, building level coaches, and administrators using the I, We, Do model and the KTL instructional practices. Once trained, the team focuses on follow-up lesson planning and review workshops, among other key pieces. This is similar to other programs, such as the National Writing Project.

The National Writing Project. The National Writing Project (NWP) is an organization that partners with higher education institutions, organizations, and communities to support high-quality writing instruction. There are over 200 local sites throughout the United States, which are codirected by faculty at local colleges and universities. This organization offers professional development, resources, research and a large selection of books in the online bookstore that encourage the teaching of writing across all grade levels.

Professional development is offered to school districts and higher education faculty. In addition, there are extensive research opportunities as well (National Writing Project, 2017). An educator taking first steps toward improving his or her personal practice in hopes of spurring on students will also find a plethora of help available. NWP is interested in changing writing from a necessary academic task of writing into an enjoyable activity through teaching mentors.

The 2015 National Writing Project Annual Report states that students involved in the College-Ready Writers Program, just one of the many offerings of the NWP, outscored control peers in four attributes of argumentative writing: those of content, structure, stance, and conventions (Gallagher, Woodworth, & Arshan, 2015). This program utilized teacher leaders who worked with classroom educators to "hone student's skills" (n.p.). Positive outcomes were noted for both students and educators who were offered "knowledge, expertise, and leadership . . . [as well as] . . . sustained efforts to improve writing and learning for all learners" (National Writing Project Annual Report, 2015).

Notable is that the College-Ready Writers Program engaged educators in over forty-five hours of rigorous professional development. Embedded throughout the year, the program offered educators a variety of learning opportunities including demonstrations, coaching, and coteaching. Additionally, educators studied "effective practices in writing instruction" (n.p.), reviewed current research, and analyzed student work. This is indicative of the offerings available from the NWP. The Western Massachusetts Writing Project is just one example of a national partner site.

The Western Massachusetts Writing Project. A local branch of the NWP, The Western Massachusetts Writing Project (WMWP) is located at the University of Massachusetts Amherst. The group offers an array of services similar to that of its parent, the NWP, to support the teaching of writing. Services include professional development and consulting services, graduate certificate programs in teaching of writing, annual professional best practices in writing conferences, as well as specific writing programs for youths and families (Western Massachusetts Writing Project, 2017).

Their mission statement reflects the important work they hope to accomplish: "to deepen individual and collective experiences as writers" (n.p.) as a way to transform teaching practice and improve learning. A lofty goal, to be sure, however, their professional development offerings reaffirm this with courses such as science literacy, curriculum design, teaching writing of a variety of genres, and supporting ELL students (WMWP, 2017).

National Council of Teachers of English. This group of twenty-five associations, foundations, and organizations focuses on "improving the teaching and learning of English and the language arts at all levels of education" (NCTE, 2017). Like other professional development organizations, this one has a full complement of resources including blogs, books, lesson plans, policy research, standards, and other topics of interest. In addition, resource kits, online webinars, consulting services, and conferences round out the needs of educators looking to improve their writing and language arts acumen (NCTE, 2017).

Each year the organization completes a national survey and reports out the results. Their most recent addition, Building Literacy Capacity: The Conditions for Effective Standards Implementation (Nelson, 2015), looks at how educators and districts are implementing the new literacy standards. Of note, the study found that in schools and districts where professional learning was consistent, the new literacy standards, especially writing—so prolific in the Common Core—were among the top five components leading to student success (Nelson, 2015). Clearly, the need for quality professional development cannot be ignored.

FINAL THOUGHTS

Federal regulations stress the importance of effective professional development for supporting excellent teacher performance and increasing student achievement outcomes (DeMonte, 2013; Green & Allen, 2015). Professional development should be specifically focused, researched-based, aligned with curriculum standards, build strong collegial relationships, and be intensive in nature (Earley & Porritt, 2014; Green & Allen, 2015).

Traditional professional development has failed to promote excellence in teaching and increase student outcomes because of the sporadic and inconsistent nature in which it has been presented (Bowe & Gore, 2017; DeMonte, 2013). There are several promising approaches to nontraditional practices of professional development, such as professional learning communities, self-study and action research opportunities, mentoring relationships, and professional development partnerships.

Professional learning communities incorporate learning through the building of collegial relationships and shared visions (Bowe & Gore, 2017). The implementation of action research provides opportunity for individual professional growth as well as meeting individual student and/or class needs (Mills, 2014; Vanassche & Kelchtermans, 2016).

Mentoring partnerships foster positive experiences through guidance and support. Mentoring relationships can consist of one-to-one or group models. Peer group mentoring offers several benefits including the building of trust, the sharing of ideas, and the modeling of collaboration and teamwork as essential skills for success (Marshal et al., 2013; Osten and Gidseg, n.d.). Finally, professional development partnerships link school districts with local colleges and universities in order to collaboratively develop, implement, and support professional development activities (Colwell et al., 2014).

The NWP was developed to support the teaching and learning of writing. The organization offers local sites across the United States, which provide professional development opportunities in many forms relative to the teaching of writing. In addition, the website delivers an abundance of helpful resources including access to ongoing research in the field of writing (National Writing Project, 2017).

POINTS TO REMEMBER

- *Professional development is mandated by federal regulations.*
- *Effective professional development opportunities have been linked to excellence in teaching skills and student outcomes.*
- *For professional development to be powerful and produce positive impacts on teaching and learning, activities must be focused, intensive, sustainable, research-based, and aligned with curriculum standards.*
- *Traditional approaches to professional development have proven ineffective.*
- *New approaches to valuable professional development include professional learning communities, engagement in action research, mentoring relationships, and professional development partnerships.*

Chapter 4

The Writing Pyramid: Starting with a Firm Foundation

The corpus on pedagogical theories for teaching writing encompass five logical and creative principles that are universally accepted as the fundamentals to effective writing: thinking, planning, structuring, editing, and revising. Each must be mastered individually before coalescing into a final product that shows proficiency. Whether crafting an analysis essay, a timed-writing test in school, or an email or social media post at home, the principles of writing remain in every genre.

There is a debate on whether genre-specific criteria are more or less effective than general-analytic criteria when breaking down essential needs derived from student work (Butler & Britt, 2011; Philippakos & MacArthur, 2016; Song & Ferretti, 2013). This argument highlights a shifting demand to teach sound principles that fit across the writing spectrum instead of centering strategies on traditional writing situations.

A new model of teaching instruction would offer context into the modern necessities of writing beyond the classroom. In other words, students need to be taught how to apply analysis, research, and argumentative writing methods in situations students have knowledge about, and when using common platforms at home or while communicating socially (Bazerman, 2016).

Since today's generation of students is writing more than any previous—through texts, emails, and social media—writing instruction must engage students in the techniques of sound writing principles that crisscross all genres of writing (Beach, Newll, & VanDerHeide, 2016). The modern struggling writer would seem more apt to study the fundamentals of a clear and concise tweet discussing a social issue than the traditional essay analyzing the nuances and symbolism of Shakespearean sonnets.

Choosing the genre-specific or general-analytic criteria might depend on the level and needs of the students (MacArthur, 2016), meaning a

31

differentiated approach may be essential to help the struggling writer. It is in that approach that a new model of teaching instruction emerges.

To understand the fundamentals of writing, and the expectations across genres, Wardle and Roozen (2012) define a vertical model of writing development, along with how "literary events" both inside and outside the classroom play a role in developing the struggling writer (Graham et al., 2012; Graham & Harris, 2016; Hudson, 2016). Mastery of a specific writing genre or situation must be put into context of how writing can be relayed, practiced, and refined across the entire literary map (Camp, 2012; VanDerHeide & Newell, 2013); sound principles of writing must be applied across this widening writing spectrum.

An essential theory that needs to be tested is the benefit of making writing assignments—especially in the early stages of learning fundamentals and strategies—relevant to the struggling writer's life. This approach broadens the student's understanding of writing as a practical art and application in life, going beyond student–teacher expectations and assessments (Bazerman, 2016). These could include writing letters to loved ones, or producing a newspaper or literary magazine to be distributed to peers at their schools (Baltar, 2012), or on the more modern writing platforms of social media or blogging sites (Luzón, 2013).

Using relatable writing genres for expression creates an engaging experience the struggling writer is more apt to work through. In time, the hope is for the struggling writer to discover the craft as a necessary tool for communication and learning (Bazerman, 2016). Zawilinski (2012) found that communication on blogs helps students increase aptitude in written communication, and to be more open to teach strategies during peer-to-peer exercises (Luzon, 2013).

Studying technological trends, Pifarré and Li (2012) suggested using these modern resources to develop a writing program with strategies and tasks that are clearly defined for a writing situation, as well as the role of the student and teacher throughout the collaborative process (Beach et. al., 2016; Tolchinsky, 2016).

THE DISCONNECT

Since the early 2000s, data suggests there has been a disconnect in how students are taught and learn to write. The most recent testing results released by the National Assessment of Educational Progress (NAEP) reveal only about one in four students in the United States can write at or above proficient levels. This may suggest a new model of teaching is needed. The struggling writer is either not getting necessary support, or is being given writing strategies or topics that are not engendering deep thinking (Fleming 2012; National Center for Education Statistics, 2012).

There may be other factors driving the statistics, namely, due to the writing process posing many challenges to students. First, the struggling writer must find specific and clear words to connect thoughts with readers while revealing a sound depth of knowledge (Adkins, 2013; Graham et al., 2013). Next, individual words must align in sentences and paragraphs that show an understanding of grammar and the nuances of language. Finally, the struggling writer must maneuver through a series of strategies to map, plan, structure, and revise these ideas (Connelly & Dockrell, 2016; Troia & Olinghouse, 2013).

The motivation to succeed can be quelled at any stage, whether due to a confusing lesson or simply writing about a topic that has little relevance to the student's life (MacArthur, Graham, & Fitzgerald, 2016). Writing proficiency means being able to work through a multitude of writing situations for a variety of audiences and purposes (Bazerman, 2016). Writing becomes an act of guiding the layman to understand complex subjects in ways that relate to the reader's life, as scientists must do when writing public blogs to communicate complicated trends (Luzón, 2013).

Following this model, any writing program aimed at reaching the struggling writer must offer strategies and adequate time to allow students to express words in ways that are personal and relevant to day-to-day life (Graham, Kiuhara, et al., 2012). The teacher is an essential piece to any writing program and must be trained to offer universal principles to writing while prescribing lesson requirements and expectations to students (McCarthey & Mkhize, 2013). Having different teachers approaching the craft using a variety of styles and expectations may be a reason for the current disconnect between students and their understanding of the writing craft (Ferretti & Fan, 2016).

Hawkins and Razali (2012) studied the past 100 years of writing instruction in elementary schools and discovered students' focus over most of that time centered on penmanship, product, and process. Curriculum trends reveal more genres of writing have emerged in recent decades (Hawkins & Razali, 2012), namely, book reports, personal narratives, and biographies. As times change, more genres should be examined that show writing as a practical skill students must apply beyond the classroom (Leu, Slomp, Zawilinski, & Corrigan, 2016). In short, students don't seem to associate what is being taught in school when applying it to the more dynamic written communication networks in life (Skaar, 2012).

Process is essential to academic writing, but changing times demand the struggling writer understand the methods of thinking while navigating a technologically advancing world. Research reveals challenges related to teachers resisting or not keeping up with new technology, as well as being constrained by mandates associated with high-stakes assessments (Leu et al., 2016). With those trends, some writers struggle because instruction is ineffective or does not target the necessary skills needed to be proficient (Myhill, Jones, Lines, & Watson, 2012).

When considering the challenges of teaching and assessing struggling writers, integrating theories of writing pedagogies are needed along with research of best practices within an integrated system (Leu et al., 2016). Essentially, different educators teaching writing in different ways must be replaced by a more universal approach to sound practices that foster confidence and competence in the struggling writer. Moving away from the cognitive perspective, the modern sociocultural perspective suggests the need for studying the complexities and differences in how the writing process is taught and assessed in classrooms (Bazerman, 2016; Beach, Newell, & VanDerHeide, 2016).

THE WRITING PYRAMID

Struggling writers would benefit from a tiered approach to help navigate through the five principles of sound writing: thinking, planning, structuring, editing, and revising (Graham & Harris, 2016; Harris, Graham, & Adkins, 2015). This framework moves students through three levels of learning: the creative writing tier promotes thinking and free expression; the argumentative writing tier teaches students how to structure those original, creative thoughts into opinions about issues relevant to modern life; and finally, the Research-Based Writing tier helps the student take a wider berth around those same issues by offering unbiased, inclusive evidence while connecting these issues to personal opinions and society as a whole.

Since the progression up through the creative, argumentative, and research-based tiers represents building blocks of thinking and performing, it will be termed The Writing Pyramid from this point on in this chapter. Fidelity to the evidence-based practices (EBPs) throughout this book can return to The Writing Pyramid as students learn new strategies and gain confidence in writing. The Writing Pyramid offers a framework to thematically teach the EBPs presented. Teachers need to adapt best practices to the needs of struggling students, using judgment on how to fit a given lesson or writing situation to a differentiated approach (Harris et al., 2015).

CREATIVE WRITING

The beginning stage of The Writing Pyramid fosters a free expression of thoughts first, and in time, opinions associated or born from those thoughts.

The struggling writer is often at odds with the craft due to emotional distress stemming from a lack of confidence in being able to conjure or disseminate ideas (Bruning & Kauffman, 2016). Offering writing as a creative outlet—expression of feelings, keeping a journal, or record of meaningful life events—positively impacts the development of the struggling writer (Bruning and Kauffman, 2016). This is why the foundation of The Writing Pyramid is creative freethinking.

Struggling writers offer more original writing and differing perspectives in classroom cultures that invite open-ended discourse and exploration of ideas without prescribed outcomes or strategies (Aukerman, 2013). These include lessons and activities, like journaling, that allow students to make writing choices related to individualized topics and purposes, along with how to appeal to audiences. This is essential for development in the struggling writer because originality, creativity, and an open imagination feel constrained when following prescribed methods of writing (National Writing Project, 2017).

The creative writing tier teaches students to think like writers through brainstorming; visualization; choosing and interpreting words and using mood, tone, and symbolic language for impact. The writing process must begin as a free-flow of creativity, where the writer engages in thinking about topics that are familiar (Troia, 2014).

The struggling student will perform with higher proficiency after discovering the craft of writing independently, and with a feeling of freedom to become engrossed in the writing process. Struggling writers thrive when focusing on thinking in this stage, including how ideas are generated and how background knowledge guides word choice that leads to a unique and valued expression of ideas. While in the creative writing tier of The Writing Pyramid, students should not feel self-conscious or boxed in, but explore thoughts with confidence while practicing the principles of thinking and planning (Troia, 2014).

Routines and repetition help students succeed in this tier. Opening class with a free-write journal exercise allows struggling students to engage in the creative writing process as a ritual. Journaling also gets students thinking about writing in a way that is nonthreatening, which enables students to be more intellectually prepared for the day's lesson. Teachers should urge students to write about any topic, in any style, and have students share work only voluntarily (Troia, 2014).

Giving students independence fosters a feeling of freedom that goes beyond academic writing. The goal is to help struggling writers discover how writing must begin as a personal pursuit of expression. Free writing gives students an opportunity to write without seeing the craft as an ultimatum, but, rather, a task that allows a confident communication of thoughts on wide-ranging topics.

Students determine and manage expectations in the creative writing tier. A sound practice is to encourage daily journaling for between ten and twenty minutes, depending on the dynamics of the class, and always with reassurance that writing is the intellectual property of the student that can be shared with friends, loved ones, teachers, or to online audiences (Troia, 2014).

The free expression of ideas is paramount in the creativity phase of The Writing Pyramid. Students should not feel constrained by writing conventions, genre, format, or audience (Troia, 2014). The focus is on helping students find a passion for expression using a creative thought process. Since this stage is heavy on metacognition, it is imperative to assess students based on effort, not the finished product.

The student should be urged to stay loose and take chances, and regularly reflect on when and how original ideas are created. After the student has confidently moved ideas onto the page during this phase, grammar lessons can be designed based on the individual needs of the writer. The rationale here is simple: the struggling writer will be more apt to practice and retain grammar rules while editing writing pieces that have been crafted with confidence (Hudson, 2016).

Beyond generating ideas, the creative writing tier teaches students to show off knowledge using basic structure formulas that entertain and inform audiences. This is the stage where a love of writing is forged, and it is essential to create a positive and encouraging environment in order for it to flourish (Graham & Harris, 2016).

ARGUMENTATIVE WRITING

With social media platforms, texting, emails, and traditional academic writing, students are increasingly using writing to leave a mark on the world. When moving into the second argumentative writing tier of The Writing Pyramid, the writer is able to use positions and proclivities about subjects of high interest, which are essential to having students respect the relevance of writing on a personal level. Once the foundation of creative thinking and writing is established, the student graduates to this more sophisticated tier of developing arguments (Ferretti & Lewis, 2013).

Argumentation is defined as a social issue or situation where individuals have a difference of opinion (Ferretti & Lewis, 2013). Criteria for each side must be acceptable by reasonable people who understand the disagreement (Ferretti & Fan, 2016). It becomes necessary then to teach the art of argumentation based on issues and situations where both sides of the argument are relevant and relatable to the struggling writer (Ferretti & Lewis, 2013).

Using the techniques to plan and visualize points learned in the creative writing phase, the LLD student, as well as the struggling student, is trained more deeply on structuring points and proofs to drive support in the argumentative writing phase. Recent testing data reveals the need for a focus on argumentative writing techniques.

The 2012 NAEP Writing Report Card (National Center for Education Statistics, 2012) showed about one in four students were deemed competent in argumentative essay writing. A need for focused research-based instruction was revealed when these essays showed inadequate support and a failure to qualify opposing points of view. This was due to "my-side bias" being commonplace in the student work (Song & Ferretti, 2013).

The argumentative writing tier enables students to practice moving ideas that influence others with support and evidence. The first stage of this tier begins with open-ended opinion pieces allowing the student to express perspectives without consideration of the other side (VanDerHeide & Newell, 2013; Ferretti & Fan, 2016). This empowers the struggling writer to understand the fundamentals of argumentative discourse by offering personal expression without limitation. Writing to persuade might slow the student from coming up with varying or countering points of views. Even in college, a study revealed students were less apt to come up with support for counterarguments when writing to persuade (Ferretti & Fan, 2016).

While drawing on sound knowledge of the argument at hand, students become more attuned to the issue and adversaries on both sides, while evaluating a resolution of differences (Ferretti & Lewis, 2013). In other words, the thinking of the struggling writer becomes more cognizant of opposing viewpoints when the passion for the argument is more open for discourse. Once the student shows a mastery of structuring a basic argument, the point and counterpoint are defined and practiced (VanDerHeide & Newell, 2013).

When the struggling writer doesn't have the capacity to understand the writing situation, performance will be affected during the planning, drafting, and revising stages of the writing process (Ferretti & Fan, 2016; Song & Ferretti, 2013). To effectively manage The Writing Pyramid, teachers need to reinforce the principles of sound writing based on topics that engage the struggling student through the process. The challenge of argumentative writing stems from the struggling writer having to draw on knowledge about an issue, seek out and address both sides, and follow the standards of structure and rhetoric without bias (Ferretti & Fan, 2016).

This phase has a sharper focus on peer critiques, and may include oral debates on issues where there are two sides. Anecdotes, figurative language, and general summaries are key practices to be learned and mastered as students build points to entice an audience to see multiple points of view

(VanDerHeide & Newell, 2013). Using these techniques, the second and third tiers of The Writing Pyramid seek to offer students methods to replace supposed wisdom with a depth of quantifiable and balanced evidence.

RESEARCH-BASED WRITING

This tier teaches students to creatively visualize and logically map out issues (as learned in the creative writing and argumentative writing tiers), then search for research to support claims. This is the most sophisticated phase in The Writing Pyramid since it requires the student to take an objective, comprehensive look at issues. In the research-based level, students learn to cite opposing perspectives on an issue, while qualifying both positions fairly to control a position. The struggling writer must first learn to use more qualifiers that contextualize the perspectives of multiple audiences (Aull & Lancaster, 2014).

Though essentially the same as the argumentative writing tier, students in the Research-Based Writing tier focus more attention on searching for bias in word choice while balancing information fairly and showing both sides evenly. Students are taught to stick to verifiable facts from reliable sources. The writing principles remain the same as the argumentative writing phase, but are layered with research from credible sources and studies to support the opinions of others. Though this takes a balanced approach and sophisticated, patient thinking, this is what state assessment tests typically require of students (Pearson, 2015).

BUILDING THE WRITING PYRAMID

Struggling writers become empowered when freely expressing opinions related to topics that are relatable (Bruning & Kauffman, 2016). The Writing Pyramid guides the struggling writer to creatively think, logically assert, and, finally, learn to cite sources for balanced proof. Working through writing in these stages helps the struggling writers find the voice of confidence professional writers convey in published work.

To guide the student through the tiers, the teacher would simply have to pick topics relevant and relatable to a particular student or class' interests. Topics could run the gamut, from what happens on social media, academic struggles, even a student's fears or hopes for the future. An empowered mindset to visualize language must be developed in the creativity phase of The Writing Pyramid, and subjects must be chosen that help the struggling writer envision and translate expertise in writing assignments.

While building on each principle learned through each stage of The Writing Pyramid, a reflection must immediately follow on how the student worked through the writing process to effectively show expertise on personal and external levels. A common motto for teaching writing is to "write what you know." This saying captures the mode of thinking that must be encapsulated in the struggling writer's mind.

Once the struggling writer learns to effectively describe topics with authority and expertise, the topics increase in difficulty and scope, which helps the student graduate into the argumentative writing and Research-Based phases of The Writing Pyramid. An example of each phase may help illustrate this point.

APPLIED PRACTICE: THE CREATIVE PHASE

Consider a topic in which most young writers share general expertise. Since most students are connected, an example could be to ask students to describe what happens on social media during a typical day. Some students will reveal expertise about cyberbullying; others will describe social media as a forum to share interests and spend time with friends. Students have free reign to creatively approach any expertise, and are urged to be specific and base observations and any subsequent commentary on personal experience.

Immediately following, students should reflect on how ideas were generated, and to celebrate the most effective idea(s) that were developed as an example of best efforts. Students should also reflect on how expertise on the topic of social media helped generate ideas, whether during brainstorming or during the writing process itself.

APPLIED PRACTICE: THE ARGUMENTATIVE PHASE

Ask students to draw a conclusion based on one or more of the observations made in the creative phase as a point to argue. The point can be simple: how social media is good or bad for teens today. Students are guided to present the information in a structure that sets up the argumentative point, then layer observational points as proof of that point.

Students may use key points or evidence generated in the creative writing phase, but each description or idea must now be centered on the argumentative writing point. Immediately following, students should reflect on how personal opinion was connected to observational proofs, and to make sure all proof supports and stays in line with the argumentative point.

APPLIED PRACTICE: THE RESEARCH-BASED PHASE

The student builds on the creative and argumentative phases by researching experts or studies related to the point and observational proofs offered. Students are taught how to incorporate these expert opinions by using quotes or offering attribution. Immediately following, students should reflect on how the expert opinions and/or studies expand and strengthen personal knowledge of the issue. Students must make sure all expert proofs or studies align to support proofs and argumentative points.

When done, the student has moved a single prompt through the three tiers of The Writing Pyramid and will see the steps taken to effectively write. The process begins by drawing on personal knowledge, tying a point to that knowledge, then supporting that point with credible experts who have more to add to further the writer's point.

FINAL THOUGHTS

Both struggling students and those with LLD benefit from a tiered approach to learning and practicing each principle of effective writing. The lowest tier encourages engagement and confidence through intuition and creative freethinking. The upper tiers promote sophisticated, logical frameworks that work in unison once that foundation of creativity has been established. Repetition is paramount in each tier as the LLD or struggling student studies and navigates each step of the writing process.

This learning model is effective when the most complex elements of writing are introduced, applied, and sequenced in a gradual release framework of each writing principle. The teacher first introduces a concept, with explicit support, then has the student work in teams. Once the principles are mastered, the student works alone to self-regulate a writing task (Graham et al., 2013). Using this gradual release inside a tiered approach of learning allows the struggling student to first learn the power of words and expression, then how each connects in a sentence.

Moving forward, that sentence connects to ideas in a paragraph, and eventually that paragraph becomes a singular building block in a long-form essay (Troia, 2014). The struggling writer must practice, repeat, and refine the fundamentals of each of the five principles of thinking, planning, structuring, editing, and revising. Along the way, samples of effective writing serve struggling writers as models for competency in each stage. As each principle is practiced and eventually combined, the writing process becomes a combination of all five principles working in agreement with one another (Troia, 2014).

While moving through the writing process, the struggling writer benefits by visualizing the principles of writing as connecting in a way that resembles a pyramid: the lower tier being a foundation of creative thinking and writing, a middle tier of argumentative writing moving those creative ideas into state opinions, and an upper tier of researched-based writing that offers credibility to each assertion. Each tier builds on its successor while the student learns the principled fundamentals of writing.

The Writing Pyramid helps the struggling student gain confidence and engagement in the creative cycle of thinking, planning, and structuring ideas, and then uses those fundamentals as the building blocks to refine and influence audiences in the editing and revising stages to fulfill the expectations of the writing assignment (Graham, Bollinger, et al., 2012; Graham, McKeown, et al., 2012; Olinghouse & Wilson, 2013). The Writing Pyramid itself becomes the hallmark of this book's purpose: to argue creative and logical ways to guide learning disabled students to achieve competence and confidence in writing, according to the evidence-based practices outlined in the chapters ahead.

POINTS TO REMEMBER

- *Mastery of a specific writing genre or situation must be put into context of how writing can be relayed, practiced, and refined across the entire literary map.*
- *Using relatable writing genres for expression creates an engaging experience the struggling writer is more motivated to work through. In time, the hope is for the struggling writer to discover the craft as a necessary tool for communication and learning.*
- *Any writing program aimed at reaching the struggling writer must offer strategies and adequate time to have the student express words in ways that are personal and relevant to day-to-day life.*
- *When students are able to draw on sound knowledge of the argument at hand, they become more attuned to the issue and adversaries on both sides, while evaluating the resolution of differences.*
- *A writing program must help the LLD student gain confidence and engagement in the creative cycle of thinking, planning, and structuring ideas, and then uses those fundamentals as the building blocks to refine and influence audiences in the editing and revising stages to fulfill the expectations of the writing assignment.*

Chapter 5

Self-Regulation: Skills and Knowledge Essential for Student Success

Effective writing demands dynamic thinking with multiple logical and creative processes blending together (Harris & Graham, 2013; Johnson, Hancock, Carter, & Pool, 2012; Troia & Olinghouse, 2013). A writing task requires the student to show mastery of grammar rules while simultaneously developing credible evidential support while simultaneously being graded on originality and brevity. The student must then build ideas inside the framework of sound structure.

In short, the struggling writer is tasked with being both the architect and builder with little practice blueprinting or constructing the fundamentals that make up effective writing. A method to effectively self-regulate writing quality is teaching self-evaluation techniques based on specific criteria outlined in rubrics (Troia, 2014). The writing process demands the writer identify and refine personal strengths and deficiencies during each step of the writing process.

Scaffolding is essential. For instance, the student must first learn to respect individual words, then sentences, then paragraphs, and, finally, longer-form essays. Lacking a progression of sound fundamentals coalesces into a model of learning that leaves the struggling writer unwilling to give disciplined efforts, which compounds into stunted growth in learning.

Ultimately, writing instruction must begin with universally agreed-upon principles that work in every writing situation: engagement, self-efficacy, reflections on skills, the foundation of grammar, and learning to be a critical reader. These universal principles are the foundations of all writing situations, even when the expectations of final outcomes change. Without knowledge of these principles, the struggling writer will not be able to self-regulate the writing process. Instead, attempting to put them into practice in complicated writing assignments will lead to frustration, apathy, and a feeling of inferiority.

INTELLECTUAL INDEPENDENCE (ENGAGEMENT)

Curiosity and inquiry are fundamentals to critical thinking, and must be the foundations to engage and empower the struggling writer. Writing must be taught as an act of personal discovery where freethinking promotes intellectual independence and expression (Council of Writing Program Administrators, National Council of Teachers of English, and National Writing Project, 2011).

Without this structure in place during writing instruction, students are guarded and may feign attempts, which impedes the student's self-regulation of essential skills. Whether working alone or with peers and teachers, the struggling writer must be given steps, strategies, and samples while practicing the craft. Asking students to memorize writing formulas may help in the short term, but ultimately slows the growth of struggling writers learning the principles of the craft. This has further ramifications: as formulas are forgotten or disregarded, the student becomes frustrated, gives minimal effort, and takes little ownership in the writing process.

Struggling students can learn to self-regulate their proficiency as writers based on a simple classroom practice: give more time to write (Graham, Kiuhara, et al., 2012). Instead of just writing for academic purposes, the struggling writer will find success in "free writing" for pleasure, be it a journal or creative collaboration with peers. Students who are given additional time to open the mental processes with focused thinking on the principles necessary to produce effective writing saw a 14 percentile-point jump in reading comprehension (Graham & Harris, 2016).

The teacher must encourage learning by finding ways to prepare students to understand writing using topics that are relevant to a student's life (Baltar, 2012). It could be a letter or an anecdotal recap of a lesson learned in life. The student must be engaged by the writing situations to recognize and take ownership of the fundamentals at work. In other words, asking a student to draw conclusions about the symbolism in a Shakespearean sonnet is scrambling student thinking when the student struggles with the fundamentals connecting, or even identifying, the parts of speech in an organized sentence.

Since students often get confused about teacher comments, or do not use them in ways that help promote learning, struggling writers must learn how to work through deficiencies without relying exclusively on suggestions from teachers (Varner, Roscoe, & McNamara, 2013). MacArthur, Philippakos, and Ianetta (2015) summarized a curriculum study focused on students who were taught how to plan, draft, evaluate, and revise while using self-regulation strategies that focused on setting goals, managing tasks, and reflecting on what was learned. Students following this curriculum wrote with more self-efficacy, which resulted in longer, more persuasive essays.

Students must learn how to self-regulate the writing process through self-efficacy, perseverance, and a willingness to adapt and readapt throughout a span of writing situations. Meta-analysis suggests students who learn how to properly self-regulate strengths and weaknesses as writers have greater gains in quality of writing (Graham, Harris, McKeown, 2013). Learning disabled/struggling students who were taught using the self-regulated strategy development (SRSD) model wrote longer and showed a deeper consideration of various perspectives after learning goal-setting and strategy interventions, which were also clear in students' planning and revising of essays (Ferretti & Fan, 2016).

An effective method used to help students begin to self-regulate writing is guiding the struggling writer to see the relevance of writing in all facets of life. Struggling students need to see writing as going beyond the classroom to help people engage socially while bringing meaning and identifying personal interests and the world at large (Bazerman, 2016). In short, the struggling student can view writing as helping people share words and ideas that promote knowledge inside and outside academia. Writing must be learned sequentially by problem-solving in various situations in life (Bazerman, 2016).

Students are writing more today than ever before, but are not connecting writing principles to personal texts, social media posts, or emails. Skaar (2012) found students only made small linkages between what is communicated online with writing assignments in school, showing little symbiosis between what is taught and how these teachings are applied with written communication in real life. College students revealed writing as a medium to maintain social relationships with one another. The three most frequent types of writing outside the classroom were texting, emailing, and sharing lecture notes from class (Pigg et al., 2014).

For this generation of students, blogging, online forums, messaging, and digital storyboards allow students to contextualize writing beyond the classroom and into the modern sphere of communication (Erstad, 2013; Purcell, Heaps, Buchanan, & Friedrich, 2013). The struggling writer will find practical purpose when moving away from the traditional pen and paper essay to write in forums outside academia. The student will be more apt to regulate writing when seeing the craft as a social tool, which helps develop and shape writing based on universal principles (Beach, Newell, & VanDerHeide, 2016).

BOLSTERING CONFIDENCE (SELF-EFFICACY)

The modern student writer is faced with changing expectations due to state-testing requirements (Troia & Olinghouse, 2013), fluctuating curriculums, and new revolutions in technology. Writing instruction lags behind these changes, and the struggling writer is often left without the necessary foundation to survive in the evolving educational environment. The teacher must customize solutions to help remediate any areas where the student struggles while helping the struggling writer diagnose problems and prescribe methods to refine strengths and overcome deficiencies.

While red ink on an essay will guide students to a point, the goal must be to have students take ownership in detecting, practicing, and building skills necessary to be proficient (Varner, Roscoe, & McNamara, 2013). In other words, the student must be given steps on how to manage and think through the writing process before being able to self-regulate personal methods of mastering the craft (Graham, Harris, McKeown, 2013).

In this way, writing must be taught through engagement, not compliance. A teacher can ask the student to study specific rules of grammar or a formula for structure, but it takes the student recognizing a personal deficiency that creates changes in bad habits. Corrective feedback is not enough. Students need to create personal measurements for success (Varner, Roscoe, & McNamara, 2013).

When the teacher returns a piece of writing with red marks pointing out flaws, the student feels inadequate, and, worse, sees teaching as an indictment on a lack of intelligence. Struggling writers who are instead taught skills that align to the principles of writing will not only find confidence as writers but will be more eager to write (Ferretti & Fan, 2016).

A lack of confidence is equally as detrimental to the struggling writer as cognitive or linguistic deficiencies (Bruning & Kauffman, 2016). Helping students regulate confidence by allowing a free expression of ideas, or to record personal observations and opinions, will allow the struggling writer to identify and self-regulate specific writing principles that were once challenging to develop or maintain.

A way to ensure the struggling writer's best effort in a writing task is to offer topics the student finds interesting, and equally as important, and has a base of knowledge to draw on while fulfilling the task and its purpose (Lee & Bong, 2014; Proske & Kapp, 2013). Journaling, personal narratives, and anecdotal writing allow the struggling writer to feel empowered and therefore maximize engagement in learning writing principles (Baltar, 2012).

Freewriting invites choice, which helps foster development in the struggling writer. The student must learn to regulate decision-making in writing, and in the early stages, asking students to adhere to strict expectations on topics, purpose, and perspective can restrict growth as creative and original thinkers and writers (Beach, Newell, & VanDerHeide, 2016). Classrooms that encourage writing as a form of free expression help the struggling writer develop alternative perspectives while fostering creative growth during writing projects (Council of Writing Program Administrators, National Council of Teachers of English, and National Writing Project, 2011). The struggling writer will also be more willing to participate when learning in an environment where there is a plethora of magazines, books, and samples of great writing on display (Tolchinsky, 2016). Whether due to emerging technologies or expectations for standardized testing, writing is moving beyond the realm of language arts (Troia & Olinghouse, 2013).

Teacher self-efficacy plays a role in the development of the struggling writer across all content areas learned in school, with recent studies revealing direct links between a teacher's success in classroom management, goal-setting, and giving students a chance to freely express opinions (Holzberger, Philipp, & Kunter, 2013). Since teachers' own confidence as writers is paramount to competence in teaching, universal writing principles guiding students become essential for the development of the struggling writer (Bruning & Kauffman, 2016).

Self-regulation can be taught, practiced, and refined when following the gradual release model known as "I do. We do. You do." The teacher demonstrates a writing principle, then allows students to work through that principle with the teacher, or in groups. After a discussion or presentation of that principle, students attempt the principle independently. The struggling writer regulates problem-solving that outlines strategies' purposes and benefits by experiencing a lesson in a way that helps the student internalize, maintain, and generalize key concepts (Graham et al., 2013).

REFLECTIONS (REFLECTION ON SKILLS)

The struggling writer must be taught to reflect on patterns of thought, as well as emotional reactions, while performing a writing task. For teachers, giving students time to reflect on these experiences during the planning, initial drafting, and rewriting phases is integral in building necessary self-regulation techniques for students learning how to move through the writing process (Graham et al., 2013). Using technology to coach, model, and allow students to see samples of other students' work also has a positive effect on a student's self-efficacy while learning the principles of writing (Roscoe & McNamara, 2013).

Reflections allow students to self-regulate anxiety and a lack of confidence by identifying moments of writing where the student felt empowered, along with an analysis of moments that fell short of proficiency. The focus on the two helps students balance the principles of sound writing in a way the teacher cannot perceive or evaluate with a grade or feedback (Bruning & Kauffman, 2016).

The struggling writer develops universal writing principles when giving a focused and determined effort, so self-efficacy solutions should be taught when learning. Building a positive learning environment may include relaxation techniques to manage anxiety, as well as guided imagery to quell any nervousness associated with a writing task (Hayes-Skelton, Roemer, Orsillo, & Borkovec, 2013).

An environment that fosters self-reliance and efficacy might blend a writing principle into a series of clustered writing assignments that combine into a final product (as a portfolio item, or to be submitted as a comprehensive grade). Throughout the writing process, the struggling writer reflects on each stage: how ideas are generated; how ideas lead to the production of a writing task; and what steps were taken while managing the production phase (Bruning & Kauffman, 2016).

Using technology to propel and engage student thinking with photos, illustrations, videos, and graphics can help the struggling writer make choices, consider a variance of audiences, and see the modes of feedback related to a multitude of writing tasks. These combine to help the struggling writer regulate how personal confidence and persistence flow into each expectation in the writing process (Bruning & Kauffman, 2016).

Students thrive when instruction engages the discovery of writing principles using goal-oriented methods, then by reflecting on each of those methods by mapping a student's ability to contextualize key concepts (Graham, Bollinger, et al., 2012; Graham, McKeown, et al., 2012). These are the foundations that help the struggling writer take the necessary action to become a stronger, more independent writer.

Here is a practical application of how using reflections can help the struggling writer self-regulate the writing process when learning a new principle of writing:

1. Give the student a writing assignment designed to test proficiency on a particular writing principle (i.e., word choice, support, organization).
2. Below the completed writing assignment, have the student reflect on the piece asking the questions: What areas do you think are strongest? What areas do you think are weakest? In a sentence or two, explain how you came up with your ideas and why some are strong and others are weak (this reflection becomes a record of whether the student's thoughts are in alignment with the lesson about to be taught).
3. Teach the student the principle that needs to be mastered, which will include various examples of strong work.
4. If possible, offer group work where students analyze samples of the principle being used well and poorly, and offer praise or solutions for these samples in a class discussion.

5. Have the student analyze whether this principle was effectively adopted when completing the original assignment in step 1.
6. Ask the student to rewrite the assignment by applying the principle in areas where it was overlooked on the first draft.
7. Have the student reflect on the thinking process that went on during the original draft, and what new way of thinking needed to be practiced while writing the final draft with the principle in mind.

When all these steps are taken, the student has samples of work along with notes outlining a writing principle that must be mastered. Combined, these artifacts show the evolution of how the student initially thought through the writing process, how the student should have thought through the writing process, and, finally, proof of the student effectively thinking through the writing process using the learned principle.

Reflections are crucial to self-regulation because they offer reference points where the struggling writer diagnoses a specific problem, then remediates the deficiency while working alone. In essence, it becomes a map for self-regulation—a line of evidence showing original thinking where the skill was not known, all the way to where weaknesses were diagnosed and fixed in samples that proved a mastery of key concepts over time.

The struggling writer is not just taught how to write but must be given approaches to self-regulate proficiencies of certain principles, including an awareness of strengths, weaknesses, and finally, methods of refining each. Though the gradual release model (I Do, We Do, You Do) is widely accepted as having many advantages, the progression in the recent example was recalibrated to help students self-regulate personal deficiencies in writing.

The new model strays from "gradual release" to follow a "rapid release" format to start, where the student tries alone first, without any assistance. This technique is used to test proficiencies of a specific writing principle without a student realizing the assignment is a diagnostic. After that initial writing assignment, the student is shown how to work through key concepts (Bruning & Kauffman, 2016), works in teams to build concepts, then gives an analysis on where weaknesses were present in the original draft. With that, the student rewrites the piece to show mastery of the principle.

Using reflections as a technique for self-regulation is effective when the student attempts a writing assignment that focuses on writing principles that have not yet been taught. The student is not told this is a diagnostic test, though it is imperative the student give his or her best efforts while thinking through the process. That is the challenge to teaching: the student not trying or giving a best effort, which leads to ineffective writing samples that don't reveal true deficiencies.

A key component to this rapid release is asking the student to reflect on the sample of writing with focused questions immediately after the first attempt: What areas do you think are strongest? What areas do you think are weakest? In a sentence or two, explain how you came up with your ideas and why some are effective and others are ineffective.

After this personal reflection, the next step is guiding the student through effective writing techniques that should have been implemented during the writing process. From this point on, the student is taught based on the traditional gradual release method: "I Do, We Do, You Do." For the "I Do" portion, the teacher presents notes, strategies, and samples of the writing principle being used well. This should include how the writer should think through the process, in addition to effective examples revealing the end result.

From there, students are teamed up to work through samples together (We Do), then offer analysis on the best examples. This should include explanations into how students thought through the process to determine the most effective samples. Finally, the student is asked to individually analyze proficiency of that technique in the original draft. With those notes in hand, the student then attempts the assignment a final time, rewriting it with the writing technique to guide the writing process (You Do).

FOUNDATION OF GRAMMAR
(GRAMMAR AND READING LIKE A WRITER)

Due to a lack of grammar training in recent decades, the current generation of educators has celebrated research suggesting a focus on grammar does not necessarily improve writing (Hudson, 2016), though research is now examining whether a return to grammar will mark improvements for struggling writers.

Recent research reveals that during early writing instruction, struggling writers learning how to spell (and work through thinking methods that enable spelling) increased writing quality (Graham & Santangelo, 2014). Students who were guided through spelling instruction also showed gains in reading proficiency.

Struggling writers must learn to become editors who are able to scan for problems in language and mechanics (MacArthur, 2016), and it is in the reflection process—through commentary from teachers, and from the student assessing personal work—that patterns of deficiencies will be discovered. The old way of "thinking globally" when revising a writing assignment is replaced with an "acting locally" approach to finding smaller errors in language choices, grammatical slips, and, over time, organizational confusion.

Learning grammar in this self-regulated manner will lead to more efficiency. As deficiencies are discovered, the teacher can assign lessons and practice surrounding specific problems the struggling writer can search for and refine in a writing task. Teaching targeted grammar skills by memorizing definitions and methods is an effective format to help students discover and apply language rules (Gwosdek, 2013).

The struggling writer learns grammar to analyze how language works (Hudson, 2016), so reflecting on samples of incorrect grammar in a student's own work will help give context in a personal way. Hudson (2016) highlighted two common methods: teacher-generated grammar examples to guide lessons, or extracting published or student-generated texts as samples for definitions and proper usages.

Whatever the method, the aim must be to give the struggling writer a deep understanding of grammar by mapping sentence diagrams of key grammatical rules and expectations (Hudson, 2016). The author argues the need for the struggling writer to first understand the essentials of individual words and the relationship of words, such as the connection between a verb and noun and the purpose of an adjective or adverb to clarify nouns and verbs, to begin to see the larger patterns of language at work.

In a classroom setting, the grammar lessons are focused on common errors; when working individually with a writer, the educator must look at the specific needs of a student to recognize and self-regulate errors (Hudson, 2016). Hudson (2016) discussed a problem with grammar teaching: the current generation of educators did not themselves learn the deeper rules of grammar in school. So at the least, the basic parts of speech and nuances of how language connects can be the standard to guide the struggling writer, even if the teacher is not knowledgeable about more abstract grammar rules.

A model breaks down the purpose of grammar lessons: teaching grammar gives students knowledge about grammar rules, which can then be applied to writing (Hudson, 2016). In essence, without the student knowing what a verb is, the student will be unable to connect it with purpose to the subject it enlivens.

Self-regulating grammar skills of struggling writers must be kept simple to boost confidence: master the parts of speech to effectively maneuver ideas with precision. For example, students might learn that the adjective is only necessary to highlight a noun's deeper essence, and an adverb does the same to incite clear action in the reader's mind. As an added benefit, identifying the purpose of each will help the struggling writer become a more focused and critical reader.

In the early years of schooling, reading and writing are distinct challenges (Costa et al., 2013), but beyond early elementary school, combining the two during instruction may foster more rapid development in the struggling writer (Shanahan, 2016). There is shared knowledge between being able to effectively read and write, namely, knowing how to think about, apply, and generate ideas and information while reading and writing, as well as being able to strategically predict, ask questions, and summarize information based on those skills (Shanahan, 2016).

Research suggests the more a struggling writer reads, the higher literacy proficiency becomes (Allington, 2014; NORC, 2013). Becoming a critical reader helps the struggling writer regulate revisions to a writing task. Just as a critical reader must comprehend, follow an organizational structure, connect ideas to prior knowledge, and calculate the verifiability of information, the struggling writer must think in these contexts while revising a piece of writing.

Focusing on the main idea and organization of text is a challenge for struggling writers, so learning to read critically will reinforce needed practice (MacArthur, 2016).

Effective methods of self-regulation include adopting and streamlining strategies that help the writer plan and ultimately produce good text, which will be the focus of the next chapter (Torrance, 2016).

FINAL THOUGHTS

It is advantageous to directly teach specific writing skills, processes, and knowledge because such instruction improves the overall quality of students' writing (Graham, Harris, & Santangelo, 2015; Graham, Kiuhara, et al., 2012). The successful teacher must train the struggling writer to slow down and think about the basic rules of word choice, effective use of the parts of speech, and putting ideas together in a coherent order.

Before learning how to write a sentence, the student must be taught to generate original ideas with effective word choice. Before mastering a paragraph, the student must learn the essentials of creating one great sentence that captures the essence of a focused subject. Before learning to write an essay, the student must learn the components that make up the organization and validity of those sentences in a comprehensible and engaging order.

Asking the struggling student to do this all at once and then trying to recalibrate thinking based on deficiencies is not only time-consuming and frustrating for the teacher but it's almost impossible for the student to grasp the underlying principles with absolute clarity. Once the student learns to write one great sentence, or one great paragraph, the student models the rest of writing based on that thinking. Along the way, the student must practice in concert with studying effective samples that model the writing process. The samples must focus on the "why" behind sound writing principles so students can conceptualize effective methods.

Simply showing the student a great sample is not enough. The struggling writer must reflect specifically on what makes the piece great, then relay that thinking when reflecting on pieces the student has written. It is inside that reflection that the teacher can see the student's understanding of writing principles based on personal measurements for success (Varner, Roscoe, & McNamara, 2013).

A powerful technique to empower the struggling writer is to give opportunities to take chances in the early stages. This includes guiding students to recalibrate their understanding of writing as not just an academic endeavor, but as an opportunity for personal growth and reflection. The current pedagogical models in K–12 demand students follow formulas without being taught the "why" behind the principles of effective writing. This diminishes the struggling writer's adherence to sound writing principles. The struggling writer complies rather than engages in the writing process, which stunts learning.

Writing is mirroring what has worked before, then learning to explore and discuss increasingly challenging topics while developing a style as a writer over time. The reflection process helps the student self-regulate writing in ways that show a progression of thinking and performing, which not only act as a roadmap of learning, but can be used to correct bad habits moving forward.

POINTS TO REMEMBER

- *A method to effectively self-regulate writing quality is teaching self-evaluation techniques based on specific criteria outlined in rubrics.*
- *Writing must be taught as an act of personal discovery where freethinking promotes intellectual independence and expression.*
- *Struggling students can learn to self-regulate their proficiency as writers based on a simple classroom practice: give more time to write.*
- *Since students often get confused about teacher comments, or do not use them in ways that help promote learning, struggling writers must learn how to work through deficiencies without relying exclusively on suggestions from teachers.*
- *For this generation of students, blogging, online forums, messaging, and digital storyboards allow students to contextualize writing beyond the classroom and into the modern sphere of communication.*
- *Using technology to coach, model, and allow students to see samples of other students' work also has a positive effect on a student's self-efficacy while learning the principles of writing.*
- *Students thrive when instruction engages the discovery of writing principles using goal-oriented methods, then by reflecting on each of those methods by mapping a student's ability to contextualize key concepts.*

Chapter 6

Pre-Writing Activities: Setting the Stage for Success

Teachers must allow time for students to pause and think about any previous experiences or expertise that can be used as evidential support in writing tasks. Brainstorming, planning, and researching are strategies that enable the struggling writer to draw on ideas with confidence and precision (Troia, 2014). Originality in writing comes when the writer is able to guide the reader to understand a subject from a vantage point that could only come from that particular writer. Professional writers do this by seizing opportunities to show expertise based on what has been learned or experienced in life.

Struggling writers often lack a depth of knowledge or life experience to draw on while writing (Golley, 2015). This is why it's essential to use brainstorming techniques that leave room for suggestions on what must be learned or researched to write effectively.

The initial thinking phase that begins the writing process may often signal students wanting to give up before even beginning to write, perhaps out of anxiety, or a feeling of inferiority. Therefore, the prewriting stage must be introduced as imaginative, open thinking: a creative contemplation that allows the struggling writer to feel empowered—not intimidated—by the writing process (Hawkins et al., 2008).

Prewriting activities develop the struggling writer by giving time and focus on how to generate ideas, plan content, then study how that preparation builds into drafting an effective essay (Graham, McKeown, et al., 2012). The need for prewriting is explained in an analogy to designing a building: just as it is faster, cheaper, and easier to sketch an architectural blueprint rather than attempting to build by trial and error with bricks and mortar in hand, developing and outlining thoughts for a piece of writing will lead to a more systematic and streamlined approach to completing a writing task (Torrance, 2016).

During planning, prewriting exercises become the blueprints while language choices and ideas become the bricks and mortar that translate how text is produced on the page (Fayol, Alamargot, & Berninger, 2012). Prewriting strategies train the struggling writer to contemplate and control complicated thought processes while generating ideas to produce proficient writing.

The brainstorming process is an essential principle to effective writing because it reveals what the struggling writer is able to write about. Even when a young writer is knowledgeable about a topic, the mind has limitations on how much information it has available to process and incorporate into a writing situation at any given time; planning in advance helps the writer keep work comprehensive, structured, and moving fluidly throughout the writing process (Torrance, 2016).

The more adept the student becomes at planning, the more efficient the student becomes at thinking in real time while writing. Once planning has been mastered, the goal is to have students come up with personalized planning approaches that work, since planning essentially teaches students how to think and navigate through writing (Vermont Writing Collaborative, 2017a). Only after mastering fundamental thinking methods that create effective writing—brainstorming, activating prior knowledge, research, and outlining—may the student be judged academically on the entirety of a piece.

Teaching pedagogies often guides students in reverse: a student is given an essay to write, and is then diagnosed on a series of individual deficiencies. More often than not, this creates frustrations for teachers having to diagnose a plethora of problems, one at a time. Then there is the problem of what to reteach. In a classroom with twenty-five students, there might be twenty-five different deficiencies present on varying levels (Culham, 2011). This slows learning since the impetus of remediation will be relevant to only some students. The struggling writer requires a more focused approach, and prewriting strategies incorporate sound writing fundamentals that help students engage in the first stage of the writing process.

There are many contributing factors working in tandem to determine a student's success in writing. These include an ability to focus, offer wide-ranging evidence related to a writing situation, and organize thoughts as an expression of knowledge (Adkins, 2013). Since writing is a complex subject that demands internal and external perspectives to amalgamate into varying expressions of creativity and logic, prewriting strategies offer approaches to stymie any chaos or confusion felt by the struggling writer. From helping students garner first thoughts to mapping out and ordering complex ideas, prewriting strategies offer practical procedures to help students get mentally prepared to write, brainstorm, visualize, activate prior knowledge, and finally, outline topics for essays (Graham, McKeown, et al., 2012; Graham & Sandmel, 2011).

Essentially, prewriting strategies guide the struggling student to think in an orderly manner. This minimizes any guesswork frustrating the student (and teacher) and replaces it with approaches that seek to empower confidence and cohesion in the writing process.

SELF-REGULATION THROUGH BRAINSTORMING

The writer struggles when suffering a disassociation between thinking and expression while writing, which leads to a feeling of insufficiency when presenting ideas. While the writer may initially know some, maybe even all, of the basic points for a piece while writing, decisions must be made as to how to express, organize, and emphasize those ideas (Graham & Harris, 2016).

Brainstorming offers students a framework to help cycle through thinking in ways that encourage more spirited and confident attempts at writing tasks. Brainstorming techniques are engaging when they are incorporated inside writing situations and activities that make students think about and discuss ideas for a writing situation (Graham & Harris, 2016).

Prewriting strategies present methods to generate original ideas, and then assist students to cross-reference those ideas to connect or argue opposing points of view. The struggling student can use graphic organizers while brainstorming to record and draw relationships between ideas (Golley, 2015; Graham & Harris, 2016).

APPLIED PRACTICE: PREWRITING

There are several practical brainstorming techniques using graphic organizers that are proven to propagate ideas and build confidence. To offer an applied practice, here are a few that work, in ascending order of complexity:

1. The A–Z Chart: This chart engages and empowers struggling writers to generate words and ideas related to a subject matter. Students use the letters of the alphabet to trigger words related to a writing topic, then begin organizing thoughts to build proofs and arguments.
2. The Sensory Chart: This "sight, sound, feel, smell, taste" chart allows struggling writers to imagine and visualize ideas that reflect expertise in writing assignments. This chart inspires students to write with an originality and confidence based on personal experience with the subject matter.
3. The Venn Diagram: This chart is for more complicated writing topics where there are two distinct sides. Students use the Venn diagram to mark what is known about each side, as well as commonalities that overlap from both points of view.

Part of brainstorming should include a section where the struggling writer lists information that must be researched or considered further in order to give a comprehensive and credible response to the writing situation. As part of the A–Z brainstorming chart, the student might be guided to write down ideas that would help better understand the subject. For example, if writing about the student's city, the list might include famous streets and buildings, sports teams, and possibly the weather patterns. It is possible, though, that the student may not know the mayor's name, or what the mayor stands for; perhaps the student doesn't know when the city was founded, or whether the city was an industrial or rural area during its dawning years.

Every graphic organizer should have a place to record what the student might need to know—to research or talk to people about—in order to become more expert on the writing topic. Leaving room under the A–Z brainstorming chart, for example, allows the student to gauge how comprehensive the research will be when maneuvering through that specific topic. Struggling writers who self-regulate the writing process show an improvement in writing quality, and meta-analyses reveal planning enhances writing performance (Golley, 2015; Graham et al., 2013).

Planning strategies should be taught early, since there is evidence that writing quality improves beginning in first grade when prewriting is emphasized (Calkins, n.d.; Vermont Writing Collaborative, 2017a; Zumbrunn & Bruning, 2013). In a study (Kiuhara, O'Neill, Hawken, & Graham 2012) of tenth graders, it was found that graphic organizers helped writers with disabilities to better strategize content. One strategy in particular the authors found useful was AIMS, which is outlined here:

A—Attract the reader's attention
I—Identify the problem for the reader to understand the issue
M—Map problem or offer background knowledge the reader will need to understand it
S—State the thesis clearly

The authors (Kiuhara, O'Neill, Hawken, & Graham, 2012) discovered that students who used the graphic organizer wrote essays that were more focused on topic, and were guided with more valid, comprehensive support. Building on the "reflections" portion of self-regulation from chapter 5, students can see the benefit of planning by offering assignments where they write two versions: the first without planning and the second right after planning.

While teaching tenth-grade LD students, Kiuhara, O'Neill, Hawken, and Graham (2012) found that before students were guided with planning strategies (including graphic organizers), most did little planning, which resulted in short essays without sufficient elaboration. After teaching students how to plan, the struggling writers consistently drafted more comprehensive essays with detailed background information to provide support (Kiuhara et al., 2012).

APPLIED PRACTICE: BRAINSTORMING

Brainstorming is a key principle to managing the writing process. To guide a struggling writer to understand this point, it's effective to have the student write on a prompt first without any brainstorming, then rewrite the same prompt a second time after brainstorming. An applied practice to guide the struggling writer to understand the necessity of planning based on the findings of Kiuhara et al. (2012) can be found in a simple exercise:

1. As a warm-up to begin class, have students spend about five minutes writing a paragraph that describes an old dog. Tell students time is short, so they have to write fast.
2. After the warm-up, introduce the concepts behind a "sensory chart," where the student takes about a minute to visualize and write down words that describe what the dog looks like, then another minute to visualize what the dog smells like. Do the same for sound and feel.
3. After completion, ask students to circle the words from the sensory chart that best capture the essence of the dog.
4. Ask students to write the paragraph again, this time giving ten minutes to write. Students should attempt to incorporate any strong words or ideas from the warm-up in step one, but to also incorporate words circled in the sensory chart, if these descriptions are relevant.
5. Have students offer a reflection on how the second draft was better, and, most importantly, how visualization, brainstorming, and planning made the piece more vivid and interesting to read.

The same process could be done a second time after asking students to create a second sensory chart to compare that old dog to its days as a puppy. This teaches the struggling writer to consider the past and present to compare and contrast a subject (dog) to what it was once like, in order to show how the dog is now. This assignment could be used as an artifact, or reference point, for a portfolio that proves the benefits of planning, which encourages student ownership in the thinking and planning processes that lead to proficiency in writing.

APPLIED PRACTICE: PLANNING METHODS

The best writers think in chunks when drawing on expertise from working memory; prewriting strategies enable a smooth transition of these ideas while developing each throughout the writing process (Graham, Kiuhara, et al.,

2012). Based on this, the authors assert elementary-school-aged children should learn planning strategies that lead to more information and higher-quality text. Troia (2014) offered three ways to boost creativity through pre-writing and thinking methods before writing:

1. Guided imagery where students are taught how to visualize events or circumstances in life—perhaps a vacation to the mountains or a beach house to describe a vista or sandy shoreline—to build strong sensory details to drive the writing.
2. Exposure to texts as samples of vivid, creative writing the student can pull from to model.
3. Direct sensory experiences, such as a taste test or having students handle and describe an object while blindfolded or within a sensory box (one in which there is only a small hole for a hand to fit through).

Since oral language activities were shown to increase listening and reading comprehension, vocabulary, rhetorical devices, and storytelling (Snowling & Hulme, 2012), brainstorming strategies that allow students to think-pair-share words and ideas may lead to a deeper understanding and advancement of support. As an application, students could fill out a graphic organizer, then share the three best ideas or words for a partner or small group to add to brainstorming sheets.

Prewriting gives the struggling writer an opportunity to consider knowledge of a given subject, and to make certain all claims, expertise, and support are evident based on past experiences and awareness of the writing situation (Troia, 2014). The author contends brainstorming and graphic organizers that delve into a writer's knowledge increase the quality of writing.

Planning should be taught as a practical tool, not as a means to map out every idea and structural point from beginning to end (Torrance, 2016). The author argues that planning means considering central ideas and proofs that will be discussed within the structure of the essay, then branching out support to offer a comprehensive response to the writing situation. Torrance (2016) believes this can be done as a prewriting exercise, or during the writing process itself, as new ideas come to light while composing a draft.

Whether strategies are used during prewriting or during the writing process itself, the struggling writer should understand that the end product will often vary substantially from the plan (Torrance, 2016). This same author suggests three ways to teach planning as strategies that can be taught exclusively or used in unison:

1. Planning can be taught to guide procedure by having students outline ideas and structural vantage points to move the ideas.

2. Planning can be taught to have students focus on specific writing procedures or goals (i.e., focusing on strong verbs to enliven subjects, or offering anecdotal proof as support of a distinct point).
3. Planning can be taught to help students set product-focused goals that will enable students to offer a comprehensive response to the writing situation.

APPLIED PRACTICE: MAPPING OUT AN ESSAY

When students are asked to map out an essay, it may be beneficial to offer a worksheet to plan words and ideas that drive key points, similar to the three planning strategies listed previously. For example, students might be asked to write about how social media harms youths today, and one of the key points for development is simply: "Students would be less distracted in school."

Instead of writing on the spot, the student takes time to map out word choice, anecdotal proofs, figurative language options, mood, tone, and cause-and-effect statements. Students would also have an opportunity to consider further research that could strengthen these points. The worksheet might look like the following (it should be noted that while this worksheet is geared for older students, the idea could easily be transformed for upper elementary students):

Point One to Prove from Thesis: "Students would be less distracted."

Answer each of the following questions to help inspire ideas that show students distracting themselves with phones at school, and how this hurts academic performance:

1. Verbs. What verbs might show your subject "students" being distracted by cell phones: _____

2. Adjectives and Adverbs. What adjectives and adverbs might show students being distracted by cell phones (attach specific nouns to the adjectives and specific verbs to the adverbs): _____

3. Anecdotes. Do you have a personal anecdote or can you create a hypothetical third-person anecdote to illustrate a scene that shows a student(s) being distracted by a cell phone in class? Bullet-point an anecdotal moment or two that shows the problem in a short scene.
   _____
   _____
   _____

4. Figurative Language. Try to come up with a few examples from the categories of figurative language below to show students being distracted

by cell phones. You don't have to come up with examples for every category (try to have one thoughtful example in three or more categories, if possible):

Metaphor/Simile _____

Personification _____

Alliteration _____

Hyperbole _____

Oxymoron _____

Paradox _____

Irony _____

Idiom _____

Onomatopoeia _____

Allusion _____

5. Mood and Tone. Are there any words or imaginary settings that could guide the reader's emotions to feel a certain way about the issue, or to suggest how you, as the writer, feel about this distraction: _____

_____

_____

6. IF/THEN Statement. Come up with a cause and effect that can be described using an IF/THEN statement. Consider the use of any figurative language, verbs, mood, tone, or anecdotal proof you just came up with as you craft an IF/THEN statement to show the consequence of phones being a distraction: _____

_____

7. Is there any information or expert studies you could research to help develop a scene or point while describing how phones distract students today? _____

_____

COLLABORATION

An effective way to work through brainstorming and planning is to give students time to generate ideas alone, then work together in teams to compare and build words and support for each point in an essay. Though collaborative prewriting activities have been shown to improve student writing, many classrooms do not use this approach (Lacina & Collins Block, 2012). Collaborative exercises for struggling writers may calm feelings of anxiety and guide students to discover new perspectives to confidently use as support in writing tasks (Bruning & Kauffman, 2016).

Cooperation with peers is essential for the struggling student to gain perspective beyond the teacher's red marks on assignments. Working with peers throughout the writing process is a proven method to improve performance and confidence in writing. Asking students to work together to plan, draft, revise, and edit papers saw a 31 percentile-point jump in writing quality (Graham & Harris, 2016).

Brainstorming in groups offers a strategic advantage. First, the struggling student who feels apathetic or incapable will see common ideas are often shared with and in alignment with that of their peers. This can be tested in the "I do. We do. You do" gradual release model. For example, begin with a simple mapping exercise where the teacher works with students to come up with ideas in a graphic organizer (I do), and then students team up to think-pair-share ideas in small groups (We do). Finally, the student works alone to refine and develop original ideas in the brainstorming process (You do) as an outline for writing.

A framework to engage students in activities that help with gathering and organizing possible ideas for writing saw a 21 percentile-point jump in writing quality (Graham & Harris, 2016). Simply put, the authors assert that graphic organizers help students record and draw relationships between gathered ideas.

GRAPHIC ORGANIZERS

To build a collaborative exercise as described above, a practical approach in a classroom setting would be to offer students an opportunity to showcase and vote on the individual student or student group that generated the best words and ideas. This activity could be labeled "A Marketplace of Ideas," where students work in teams to come up with words and strong support related to a writing task, then illustrate these ideas in a graphic organizer such as a sensory chart or A–Z chart.

Students are then given the opportunity to do a "gallery walk," where teams walk around the room to take notes on the words and ideas generated from other groups. Students can either be given fake money to "buy" words and ideas to then be used while writing, or encouraged to do a simple hand vote of the top three ideas presented in the gallery walk as a suggestion for what the class should be required to incorporate into a writing piece. This shows the struggling writer the process is fluid, and the approach to a specific piece of writing can be guided by myriad vantage points.

Again, a practical approach to using brainstorming includes having students share ideas in groups to create a presentation of ideas for display. Brainstorming in groups, then presenting the findings of each, allows struggling writers to borrow from the "Marketplace of Ideas," which helps reinforce the foundations of great writing: deep thinking, researching, and seeking out original ideas to present to an audience. After meeting the standard in a team, students will have increased confidence to come up with original ideas.

PERSONAL EXPERIENCES

Drawing on personal experiences is a principle to great writing that must be practiced and mastered in the prewriting phase. It is essential to offer students opportunities to write about engaging, personal topics in which they can visualize the writing; thus, boosting their confidence levels considerably (Baltar, 2012). Struggling writers will take more ownership in prewriting strategies when the writing activities are built around paragraphs and essays that cover topics of high interest.

Topics such as whether cell phones should be banned in school, the problems of social media, or even relationships with peers and adults are all topics that may be considered. After practicing brainstorming techniques that activate prior knowledge, the struggling student will be better equipped to build arguments around personal experiences and knowledge related to these subjects.

SENSE OF PLACE VISUALIZATION

In later stages, prewriting exercises can be used to help students connect ideas to a common theme that can be carried in a piece of writing. It is important to offer students topics that garner high interest, and which the students have a basis of knowledge on, so the ideas can be plentiful to draw from, and in doing so, connect themes (Lee, Lee, & Bong, 2014; Proske & Kapp, 2013).

APPLIED PRACTICE: PERSONAL EXPERIENCE

An applied practice of this strategy would be to ask students to describe a place that is familiar, such as a bedroom or classroom. The student would fill out an A–Z chart or sensory chart, then look for commonalities in the word choice that could add up to a specific theme. This not only helps the struggling student generate ideas through brainstorming but also begins to add up those ideas to a singular thematic purpose when writing the piece. Better, figurative language, mood, tone, and anecdotal writing could be taught in this context to help the student use the graphic organizer to develop a theme to describe the room.

Let's say a student is describing a classroom. The student would complete an A–Z brainstorming chart to begin. Based on the words that arrive, the student would then search for a theme based on the preponderance of word choices being positive or negative in nature. In other words, if the student uses words that show a militant, stiff classroom atmosphere, that becomes the theme, and each detail must follow that theme with that purpose in mind.

Every detail, each word chosen, and even grammar choices add up to create the ambiance. Doing this by having students write about a familiar setting raises engagement and success in learning an essential principle. Once the theme is chosen, the writer simply uses the key words that convey the theme. This reinforces how brainstorming can act as a guide to writing. While the assignment's topic may seem low level, the creative visualization and theme building will guide the student to write with a more sophisticated purpose.

As always, allow students to reflect on the process of how brainstorming leads to developing words that connect to the theme and underlying purpose of writing. This prewriting strategy is also a method to assist students who often put in miscellaneous details that veer off point. As all writing does, learning to craft a piece with a calculated focus will help the struggling writer become a better reader, by learning and practicing choices to convey messages.

FINAL THOUGHTS

The struggling writer may approach the craft with any number of negative thoughts. Some feel diminished; others feel incompetent; most feel flustered and confused (Golley, 2015). This may make the student not want to try, which compounds to create a bigger problem: teachers are not working with a student's best efforts. In short, remediation gets entangled in student apathy bred from insecurities. A subtle fix to this problem exists by making the writing environment creative rather than threatening. The prewriting phase is the time to instill a creative spirit in developing writers (International Literacy Association, 2017).

These approaches attempt to recalibrate any ineptitude students feel when beginning the writing process. Once prewriting strategies are adjusted to maximize productivity while learning, the teacher may begin unpacking writing practices to build on that engagement. Disciplining struggling writers to use simple planning techniques increases expertise in writing, which empowers the student to want to work more vigorously through the writing process.

Struggling writers must learn that writing is a reflection of knowledge, and that mastering techniques to draw on that knowledge is an essential first step to engage and broaden thinking. This seems intuitive, since most young writers who resist planning and mapping exercises admit the writing process is smoother, more inspired and original after careful planning (Graham & Harris, 2016).

Planning takes time, and demands discipline, but guiding the struggling writer to effectively plan is a key to diagnosing how the writer thinks. The struggling writer will find further incentive after mastering the techniques and realizing words arrive with more confidence while writing. All writers, seasoned or new, eventually hit a limitation on knowledge and run out of ideas to present. The experienced writer knows this is the time to read more on the topic, dig into research, or talk to experts in the field related to the topic being covered (Graham & Harris, 2016).

Part of creative visualization should include asking students to consider relationships to topics by comparing them to other topics with similar characteristics. Figurative language helps struggling writing connect to the topics they write about, which deepens engagement in the writing process. Leaving a section of a creative map for metaphors or similes will help the struggling writer find confidence in generating original ideas. This can help the struggling writer realize that effective writing is the result of learning how to effectively think through ideas.

POINTS TO REMEMBER

- *During planning, prewriting exercises become architectural blueprints while language choices and ideas become the bricks and mortar that translate how text is produced on the page.*
- *Planning in advance helps the writer keep work comprehensive, structured, and moving fluidly throughout the writing process.*
- *Prewriting strategies offer practical procedures to help students get mentally prepared to write, brainstorm, visualize, activate prior knowledge, and, finally, outline topics for essays.*
- *After learning prewriting techniques and planning, students consistently draft more comprehensive essays with detailed background information to provide support.*
- *Prewriting gives the struggling writer an opportunity to consider knowledge of a given subject, and to make certain all claims, expertise, and support are evident based on past experiences and awareness of the writing situation.*
- *Collaboration during prewriting exercises may calm feelings of anxiety and guide students to discover new perspectives to confidently use as support in writing tasks.*

Chapter 7

Writing Structure: Underscoring the Importance of the Framework

Instruction that encapsulates the fundamentals of structure can be introduced by breaking down the essentials of a paragraph: how to create an engaging topic sentence, driving for deeper impact when concluding ideas, transition clauses and sentences that move points, and valid support that influences audiences (Troia, 2014). The author asserts a well-formed paragraph can be a model for more complex, long-form structural components, incorporating a small piece of what the entire essay must encompass. In this way, structure is essentially making certain a central idea is clearly propositioned with valid support to move that idea in a coherent, organized fashion.

Teachers must use universal terms when presenting the fundamentals to sound structure. Important terms that need to be practiced early and built upon include the thesis sentence, topic sentence, support, transitions, and concluding sentences. Students who are given varying definitions and expectations of these structural components may become confused, and, worse, are not building on previous knowledge necessary to delve into more dynamic and complicated structural formulas.

Students will struggle to learn the fundamentals of structure in long-form essays if the components of a clear, unified sentence have not been mastered, which is why teaching grammar with a focused approach to individual student needs can build the foundation for writing (Hudson, 2016). Teaching the components of a masterful sentence—strong subject-verb connection, descriptive words to emotionally engage the audience, clarity to make sure the idea will be understood by most readers—is principal to being able to guide the struggling writer to layer those same ideas in that coherent, organized fashion that makes up structure.

In essence, teaching a struggling writer how to write one great sentence will become a model for how to craft a great paragraph, which will become a model on how to layer ideas throughout a meaningful essay that shows structural proficiency.

When structuring an argumentative writing piece, the struggling writer must be taught how to contextualize and recontextualize proofs and claims based on the perspectives and counterarguments from adversaries as a way to establish credibility in being able to manage a variety of viewpoints on an issue (Beach, Newell, & VanDerHeide, 2016).

A challenge with teaching structure may result from writing prompts that do not task students with thinking about deep, multilayered responses to writing situations. Researchers analyzed 222 prompts from writing assessments in forty-four states and found about two-thirds offered students little choice when addressing the topic or writing task, about half did not clearly identify an audience, and 22 percent gave the stance students were expected to take (Olinghouse, Zheng, & Morlock, 2012).

A reason for simplified writing prompts may include assessors struggling with valid and reliable rubrics that consider a student's voice while taking a stand on an issue (DiPardo, Storms, & Selland, 2011). More complex prompts will come when rubrics are created that focus more on how students contextualize and engage in a variety of perspectives while writing (Beach, Newell, & VanDerHeide, 2016).

There is not a preponderance of research (Beach, Newell, & VanDerHeide, 2016; DiPardo, Storms, & Selland, 2011; Olinghouse, Zheng, & Morlock, 2012) in guiding the struggling writer on structure; so applied approaches will offer support in this chapter. From rubrics, modeling, and planning strategies to approaches for introductions, conclusions, and generating ideas, this chapter will include tools and formulas to guide the struggling writer to envision structure as a process to build sound writing principles.

ESSAY STRUCTURE CHECKLIST

Checklists and questioning techniques to help in structural revisions and editing of prompts are principal elements in classrooms (Troia 2014). An applied practice to help the struggling writer overcome and manage the elements of a rubric that focuses on choice, audience, and the validity of points is to diagram those elements of structure (thesis, topic sentences, transitions, support, closing sentence), to show the student's understanding of each. For example, for the five-paragraph essay, students may be given a checklist to go in line with rubrics outlining more specific expectations for a given writing task:

Introduction with Thesis

[ ] The essay has a central idea and between two and three points attached as proof. It is written with action verbs that pop, specific and thoughtful word

choice, including adjectives and adverbs that are 100 percent necessary to further the central message.

Body Paragraph One

[ ] Opens with a topic sentence and a central idea that is clearly stated using action verbs, specific words, and adjectives and adverbs that are 100 percent necessary.

[ ] Has several sentences that "show" and build on the central idea of the topic sentence with clear, logical, and creative examples that use strong verbs, adjectives, adverbs, and specific words.

[ ] There are transition words and phrases to help the reader move between distinct ideas.

[ ] There is a closing sentence summarizing the central idea in a unique way (IF/THEN statements work well, as do all cause-and-effect recaps).

Body Paragraph Two

[ ] Opens with a transition clause putting the main idea from the previous paragraph to bed to then awaken a new central idea offered in the new topic sentence.

[ ] The topic sentence has a central idea that is clearly stated using action verbs, specific words, and adjectives and adverbs that are 100 percent necessary.

[ ] Has several sentences that "show" and build on the central idea of the topic sentence with clear, logical, and creative examples that use strong verbs, adjectives, adverbs, and specific words.

[ ] There are transition words and phrases to help the reader move between distinct ideas.

[ ] There is a closing sentence summarizing the central idea in a unique way (IF/THEN statements work well, as do all cause-and-effect recaps).

Body Paragraph Three

[ ] Opens with a transition clause putting the main idea from the previous paragraph to bed to then awaken a new central idea offered in the new topic sentence.

[ ] The topic sentence has a central idea that is clearly stated using action verbs, specific words, and adjectives and adverbs that are 100 percent necessary.

[ ] Has several sentences that "show" and build on the central idea of the topic sentence with clear, logical, and creative examples that use strong verbs, adjectives, adverbs, and specific words.

[ ] There are transition words and phrases to help the reader move between distinct ideas.

[ ] There is a closing sentence summarizing the central idea in a unique way (IF/THEN statements work well, as do all cause-and-effect recaps).

Conclusion

[ ] Has a transition followed by a reinvention of your thesis, with a focus on the future, the smartest solution, the funniest or most ironic part of your message, what wisdom the reader should take away, or a famous quote related to your topic.

[ ] Has specific ideas that further recap and address this reinvented thesis.

[ ] A final sentence that offers a rhetorical question, observation, or guess for the future that has a deep consequence related to addressing the central point covered within the essay, or the danger of not considering the many sides described within the arguments.

IMITATION GAME

One of the principles of writing is building on what has been written before, so imitation using anchor sets is a sound method to teaching structure. The benefit is twofold for the struggling writer: anchor sets become models to draw original ideas and ways of expression for a particular writing task; during an analysis of the models, the student becomes a more critical reader looking for the components of sound writing to "borrow" from. Giving anchor sets that allow students to mimic writing fundamentals will improve writing, even if students seem to be "copying" portions.

Though this may be low level at first, having students tag the components of a sentence (transitions, word choice), along with elements in a paragraph (topic sentence, support of the topic sentence, concluding sentence), can be used to test a student's ability to recognize the fundamental building blocks of a cohesive paragraph.

An effective anchor set will include tags of the components mentioned previously, as well as offer an analysis of what makes the writing effective beneath. Simple discussions on these points can help students in the initial phases, but offering hard copies for students to study and model will increase engagement and learning.

Here is an example of the practice applied. In this example, students were asked to argue why cell phones should be banned from schools. The paragraph before this argued a ban would reduce distraction, while this paragraph carries the next point, namely, teachers would not have to waste time policing cell phones during learning time. Students could be given this sample, along with the tags, to use as a model and study the parts of an effective paragraph:

Maybe more important than fixing the distraction problem (transition clause to close out previous point about "distractions"), teachers would benefit because they would no longer have to act as undercover detectives in classrooms filled with technological criminals trying to steal time away from learning (topic sentence using figurative language to illustrate the point). As a result (transition into proof of topic sentence), students who respect learning would stop losing to the cat and mouse game that is robbing them of intellectual discovery. Moreover (transition into further proof of topic sentence), teachers dealing with cell phone violations know a ban would allow them more crucial time to prepare students for state tests that are often graduation requirements. Consequently (transition into further proof of topic sentence), administrators should demand a ban, since a lower performance on state tests suggests they are unable to manage academic success in their schools. In the end (transition into further proof of topic sentence), the time teachers spend battling students over phones could be used to promote the real reason everyone should show up to school each day: to learn. More importantly (transition into further proof of topic sentence), a ban would keep teachers relaxed and ideas moving more fluidly, and administrators could rest easy knowing students are developing the knowledge and skills needed for academic success. Added up (transition into concluding sentence as proof of topic sentence), if teachers are expected to police cell phones, they are doing little more than training students to be clandestine criminals finding creative ways to breach the system (concluding sentence that draws on cause and effect to address potential consequences of not addressing the issue).

This sample enables students to see how to effectively argue a point in an essay while applying the fundamentals in a well-written paragraph. This can be used to offer the struggling writer ideas to draw from, but, more important, help guide students to move those ideas from opening line to concluding sentence. Offering practical models of well-structured paragraphs will enable the student who is confused or intimidated by where to start, where to go, and start filling the blank page with words that follow a recognizable set of structural points that lead to proficiency.

TRANSITIONS

Transition word banks should be given to the struggling writer with categories: emphasis, time sequence, support, counterpoints, and concluding points. Once students recognize transitions are needed when changing subjects from paragraph to paragraph or even sentence to sentence, blank lines can be incorporated into a paragraph when there is a subject shift (with a subsequent transition word bank), for the student to recognize where and what kind of transition will best fit the writing situation.

When the bell rings to open class each morning, students' eyes are not watching the teacher giving instruction, but are gazing at devices hidden in their laps where they tweet, scroll, and post their academic futures away. _____ every school should care about this distraction, especially if it wants to establish a respect for learning and a reputation for excellence in the community. _____, society demands a fix to this problem since an educated workforce will help ensure a prosperous future of innovation, research and culture. _____, banning cell phones would push students to be more engaged in learning, and teach them the discipline of putting away distractions while thinking about important topics. _____, this simple act will ensure an educated public that is more innovative and creative because this rising generation of students is better educated. _____, if students are given free reign to use their phones during class, then this emerging crop of students may become a generation of dunces who can't think for themselves or the betterment of society.

Offering students the answers immediately following an exercise on structural components enables the struggling writer to reflect on responses to bring clarity and remediate misunderstandings. For the previous exercise, the student might be given answers such as this:

1. This is why
2. Furthermore,
3. Without a doubt,
4. Moreover,
5. In the end,

Your paragraph might look like this, though there are other options. Each paragraph will contain transition words to help the reader experience the point of the story better or move the story more smoothly from subject to subject as points are made throughout the paragraph.

GENRES

Students must systematically learn about various genres in writing to understand there may be variations to structure. Depending on a genre (i.e., narrative, informational, persuasive), the student will have to incorporate different approaches to initiating and moving ideas within the writing task.

For example, a piece intended to entertain may open with an anecdotal recap of a situation, or an observation that is humorous to the reader, while the structural components to open a piece to inform may weigh the most relevant facts to be discussed at length later in the piece. Students could read a blog posting of a timely social debate versus a *New York Times* newspaper story about the same and determine the different strategies used to convey and disseminate the information.

Offering pieces that have different approaches (the blog opens with an opinion, whereas the news story opens with the most relevant facts) allows students to analyze various genres for informative versus argumentative writing prompts. Kiuhara et al. (2012) used STOP, DARE, and TREE strategies to develop structure, which increased students' planning and writing time, and led to higher-quality essays that had more support and background knowledge illustrating multiple points of view.

STOP: Suspend judgment, Take sides, Organize ideas, Plan to adjust as they write

DARE: Develop thesis, Add ideas to support their proof, Reject arguments on the other side, End with a strong conclusion.

TREE: Tell what they believe (state a topic sentence); Reasons (three or more reasons for believing this); End it (wrap it up right); Examine or Explain (make certain I have all my parts and make sure each reason has proper evidence)

Depending on the writing situation, the struggling writer can build opinions, facts, and supporting evidence using one of these strategies. In doing so, structure is offered by layering information based on the needs of each step, then by offering transitions to move points and counterpoints required within specific writing genres.

WRITING CONCLUSIONS

Experienced writers give context to writing based on a wider scope of rhetoric to generate central ideas and proofs (de Milliano, van Gelderen, & Sleegers, 2012), which is essential to adding up themes to maximize impact when presenting a conclusion. Writing conclusions in this way helps the struggling writer gain a "global context" that guides the expectations and acceptance of a wider range of audiences, which is a component that is lacking in argumentative writing assignments according to recent testing data (Song & Ferretti, 2013).

When crafting conclusions, the struggling writer often mirrors what was written in the introduction. Instead, students must be taught strategies on how to reinvent the central idea and points to prove it in a provocative way. A way to begin guiding students on this principle is to use graphic organizers, sentence stems, and questioning techniques that readdress the subject from a unique vantage point.

An effective method that helps the struggling writer develop context to the conclusion is when answering the question "So what?" to drive into a final recap on what was written. In other words, the student is guided to consider what the opening paragraphs to that point add up to in relation to the larger consequence. If that approach is added up effectively, the conclusion will reinvent the message. For students who continue to struggle with the conclusion, consider giving exercises where the conclusion is written first. This helps the struggling student see what the piece is driving toward at the beginning of the writing process.

Another technique to help the struggling writer contextualize a more sophisticated conclusion is to ask guided questions about the topic under discussion. The student should start out from a wide perspective, then come closer to discuss more specific impacts on a situation.

Here are some questions the student can answer to begin formulating a strong response:

1. How would addressing the situation I'm writing about affect people living on the planet?
2. How would addressing the situation I'm writing about affect just the people living in the United States?
3. How would addressing the situation I'm writing about affect just the people living in my state/city/school?
4. How would addressing the situation I'm writing about affect just a specific subset of people (i.e., teens)?

There are also sentence stems the student may use to rewrite the thesis and develop points inside the concluding paragraph. These stems include looking to the future, a smart solution, an ironic or funny message, wisdom the reader should take away, or opening with a famous quote or idiom that relates to the subject in some way. The student can incorporate the writing situation inside the blank lines and begin to reformulate the central idea argued up to that point. Here are some examples:

In a sentence or two, what does all you wrote mean for the future?

Transition Stem One: Added up, the future of the world/society/this generation depends on _____ if it expects _____.

Transition Stem Two: Looking to the future _____ must happen or the world/society/this generation will experience

_____.

Transition Stem Three: As time moves forward, the world/society/this generation must join together to _____ or be faced with

_____.

In a sentence or two, what is the smartest solution to solve this problem?

Transition Stem One: It's time for the world/society/teenagers to _____ _____ in order to help solve _____.

Transition Stem Two: Even the most foolish person can see _____ must happen if _____ is going to be prevented in the world/society/teenage realm.

Transition Stem Three: Added up, the solution is simple: _____ has to be addressed if _____ is going to be avoided in the world/society/among teenagers.

In a sentence or two, what is the funniest or most ironic part of your message?

Transition Stem One: Added up, it's ironic that _____
_____, though the world/society/teenagers can't forget _____.
Transition Stem Two: Looking at the big picture, it might seem comical that
_____, though it's dangerous to forget _____.
Transition Stem Three: While _____ may seem funny/
cute on the surface, it would be a mistake if the world/society/this generation overlooked _____.

In a sentence or two, what wisdom should the reader take away from what you wrote?

Transition Stem One: Without careful consideration of _____, the
world/society/this generation will suffer _____.
Transition Stem Two: All told, being educated on _____ can
only help the world/society/this generation to _____.
Transition Stem Three: Paying mind to _____
is essential for the world/society/this generation to _____.

In a sentence or two, tie in a quote (or idiom) that follows the theme in relation to the central idea of your piece.

Transition Stem One: In the famous words of _____,
" _____."
Transition Stem Two: Added up, maybe the world/society/this generation
needs to heed the words of _____ who said,
" _____."
Transition Stem Three: In the end, _____ may have
understood this problem best when he said, " _____."

ANECDOTES

Baltar (2012) described how the struggling writer must be engaged in the
writing process to master the principles of effective writing. One practical method that can guide the struggling writer is using anecdotal writing
opportunities to practice structure and building support around a central idea,
which can help students engage in a variety of viewpoints in writing (Beach,
Newell, & VanDerHeide, 2016).

Following the author's advice, anecdotal writing helps the struggling
writer ascertain through visualization how effectively different points can be

presented or argued in a piece. The anecdote engages the struggling writer to pinpoint and expand knowledge of a given topic, which becomes the basis for thinking when developing more complicated writing assignments.

Essentially, the anecdote is a short story that is built around a specific point, or epiphany, related to the story's theme. For example, if discussing a time when the student had to tell or was told a white lie, the student could add up that experience to guide a comprehensive central idea: "It's never a good idea to tell a lie, even if it seems harmless, because it can lead to unexpected consequences." Or, "Sometimes it's okay to tell a white lie if it's intended to protect someone's feelings."

These specific points are essentially mini theses, where the anecdote itself becomes the support to show the struggling writer's wisdom surrounding the deeper theme or epiphany gained. Better, since the prompt is centered on a single idea of a lesson learned based on a short scene to prove that point, the student could begin by writing the lesson learned or go in reverse and write the anecdote itself, then build the lesson learned after. This facilitates both types of learners: the logical learner who must have the point up front to then develop the anecdote, as well as the creative learner who prefers to write wider and with more freedom, then add up the result with a logical connection.

All of this teaches structure, but in a way that is easily understandable and relatable. Building on this, the struggling writer can better diagnose when moments in the anecdote itself veer away from the central point the anecdote is centered on. Since the anecdote is personal in nature, the struggling writer can easily spot where any moments in the anecdote stray from the central message.

The thesis sentence of a more complicated writing task must do the same, but with multiple points to be defended with support in the body paragraphs. Teaching simple structure based on a two-paragraph essay (thesis in one paragraph, the anecdote in the other) helps the struggling writer see structure on display in a manageable writing situation.

Anecdotal writing offers three benefits to the struggling writer. First, it increases confidence in the student's ability to write with originality based on personal expertise, which facilitates learning in the writing process (Ferretti & Fan, 2016). Second, it offers needed practice into building support around a central idea. Finally, the anecdote helps students make sure support proves a central idea, which offers needed practice for students who lack a focused approached to writing.

Once mastered, the same two-paragraph anecdote and thesis can be used to show the counterargument in a writing situation. Building on the examples above, the student who suggests telling a white lie is okay can begin to consider how the other side views the situation. This approach gives the struggling writer a way to gain context in simplified writing prompts that can be modeled as the principles of structure are learned and practiced. These become the models for success while moving into more complex writing situations.

Finally, when developing a more complex thesis statement with a central idea and multiple points to prove it, the struggling writer can be guided to create a hypothetical anecdotal scene that visually depicts these points in the thesis. For example, imagine a student arguing social media is bad for teens today (central idea) because it distracts students at school (point one), is a source of cyberbullying (point two), and disturbs students' sleep and health because so much time is spent on the platforms (point three).

After developing that thesis with this central idea and three points attached to prove it, the writer should open with a hypothetical scene that shows a young person being distracted, maneuvering past cyberbullies online, and feeling sleep deprived and/or a deterioration of health due to too much time spent engrossed by social media. Anecdotal scenes, even when imagined, help the struggling writer gauge how well points can be argued showcasing visual examples based on expertise.

THESIS AND TOPIC SENTENCES

The introduction of any piece offers a clear, broad summary of a central idea(s) that is addressed using smaller, focused proofs inside the body paragraphs and conclusion. Whether it's an argument, analysis, or expository essay, the first paragraph or two must define, describe, or declare, using broad language, what the rest of the essay will cover in more specific detail. A practical approach to explaining the thesis is to break it apart incrementally into a logical framework.

The struggling writer can find confidence in writing a thesis when it's created through questioning techniques that seek to answer the central point that will be explored. Since the five-paragraph essay is often taught in schools, here is a three-step formula students can work through to draft a thesis with three distinct points:

Step One: What is the central idea the essay will discuss, in general terms? To answer this, broadly describe the problem or what will be argued, if the essay prompt asks students to take sides.

Step Two: Bullet-point three unique points of evidence that could be used as points to support the central idea based on the description or position taken in Step One.

Step Three: Extend the central idea in Step One by adding the three points that were brainstormed in Step Two. When complete, the result should be an unpolished thesis, but that's enough to get the rest moving.

Brainstorming ideas to offer support to a central idea in this fashion allows the struggling writer to determine the validity and strength of the thesis. In other words, if the student is unable to come up with points and support in the brainstorming process, it will save time by not discovering that fact while writing.

One way to begin brainstorming is to develop topic sentences that drive the evidence to be proven in body paragraphs. Students can promote originality by writing multiple topic sentences using sound principles. One technique is to present the point using anecdotal writing. A second would be to present the point using figurative language. Finally, students could use a general summary, as is traditionally learned in English classes.

Once the thesis and topic sentences are planned, questioning techniques can guide students to build support around both. Students can use brainstorming charts or just answer the following questions on a planning sheet to map out support of each piece of evidence. When considering answers to these questions, the student should write in complete sentences. In that way, part of the piece is being written while planning, which saves time and helps the struggling writer see a more streamlined purpose to planning. Essentially, here are two questions the student should seek to answer while building support around a claim:

1. Who, specifically, should care about the point in the thesis and/or topic sentence and why?
2. Who, specifically, will benefit if the problem in the topic sentence is addressed or fixed and how?

From there, the pieces of the topic sentence and answers to those two questions are stacked on top of each other. This minimizes the challenge of having to pay attention to all the moving parts that make up a paragraph. Instead, each is practiced one after the other until the principle of structure becomes instinct. Finally, if the cause-and-effect sentence is mapped out on the brainstorming sheet, the student can transfer that sentence to the bottom of the paragraph as a closing sentence. When looking at structure in pieces, the process becomes simpler while practice becomes more fluid. There are any number of techniques that can be used to address structure, but focused attention and questioning are methods that move the process in a simple, engaging way for the struggling writer.

FINAL THOUGHTS

Struggling writers don't have a hard time grasping structure. The confusion comes when becoming distracted or not mapping out how ideas should be stacked inside cohesive formulas. Teaching the parts of speech, anecdotes, specificity in writing, mood, tone, and figurative language takes far more processing than structure, but structure is often taught first without having the basic principles of language in place.

A problem with teaching writing is there is no fail-safe method on how to approach the craft. Because of this, terminology gets mixed up and is not streamlined into every classroom. A consideration of this point can be discovered when talking about the components of the thesis sentence and topic sentences. The two are not taught and practiced with universal definitions, though they are essential principles to learning the structure process.

In order for structure to work, each tool guiding the student through the writing process must be carefully and consistently defined. For example, the thesis sentence must always be defined as the central idea of a piece of writing with some number of points attached to prove that central idea. The topic sentence is defined as the central idea of a given paragraph, which goes in direct line with one of the points attached to prove the central idea of the thesis sentence.

Those definitions are confusing to a degree, which proves the need for consistency when defining each. More importantly, applying those definitions to the writing process must be practiced in easy-to-understand exercises. Anecdotal writing is one of the most effective ways to develop the essentials of the thesis and topic sentences.

Since students verbalize anecdotes to friends and family members daily, transferring them onto the written page should feel natural. The key is to explain that anecdotal recaps spanning a minute, hour, month, or year must hinge on a point, which becomes like a mini thesis. In this way, the student learns what a thesis and topic sentence are in theory, but by using each in applied practice.

Finally, using questioning techniques, sentence stems and organizational strategies that follow prescribed methods of stacking information all offer tools for the struggling writer to contextualize structure. Offering checklists and other tools that help structure effectively can be modeled to engage and empower the struggling writer's efforts. Structure then stops becoming a logical framework, but rather a way to enhance creative ideas that help the struggling writer feel a connection to writing as a means of critically communicating ideas.

POINTS TO REMEMBER

- *Students must be guided to learn the essentials of a paragraph: how to create an engaging topic sentence, driving for deeper impact when concluding ideas, transition clauses and sentences that move points, and valid support that influences audiences.*

- *When structuring an argumentative writing piece, the struggling writer must be taught how to contextualize and recontextualize proofs and claims based on the perspectives and counterarguments from adversaries as a way to establish credibility in being able to manage a variety of viewpoints on an issue.*
- *Researchers analyzed 222 prompts from writing assessments in forty-four states and found about two-thirds offered students little choice when addressing the topic or writing task, about half did not clearly identify an audience, and 22 percent gave the stance students were expected to take.*
- *Researchers used STOP, DARE, and TREE strategies to develop structure, which increased students' planning and writing time, and led to higher-quality essays that had more support and background knowledge illustrating multiple points of view.*
- *Anecdotal writing opportunities help students practice structure and building support around a central idea, which can help students engage in a variety of viewpoints in writing.*

Chapter 8

The Necessity of Editing: Strategies to Guide the Revision Process

The struggling writer must learn to become cognizant and critical of creativity, word choice, and credible support to drive key points proving a central idea. Editing strategies empower the struggling writer to identify, diagnose, and resolve any deficits that occur during the writing process (Golley, 2015). While writing, the student must focus attention on the following: generating new information, structuring the information available, and rereading and refining text that is already written. This three-step process can happen simultaneously while writing a sentence or paragraph, but without the foundation of the first two, rereading text with a critical eye for improvement may be challenging for the struggling writer.

Teacher feedback, peer reviews, instruction in goals and strategies, offering students evaluation criteria, and enabling students to observe readers evaluating text all increase competency in revision and overall writing quality (MacArthur, 2016). Revision techniques help the student self-regulate the writing process, and have been proven to help the struggling writer improve proficiency in the final draft (Graham et al., 2013).

Students who revise often in the early stages of the writing process may struggle in getting started, or have difficulty grasping the task, tone, style, or focus of the assignment (van den Bergh, Rijlaarsdam, & van Steendam, 2016). Conversely, the authors assert that the student who revises at the end of the writing process does so to align the text to the goals of the writing task. Revision is traditionally the time when a student reflects on and concludes the writing process, but if a student revises ideas and sentences in the beginning, the teacher may prescribe prewriting exercises to help streamline the production of a workable draft for revision.

Students today must learn to distinguish writing as a social expression among peers online with expectations in the classroom and all of academia

(Dyson, 2013). This generation of students is faced with having to learn to differentiate between appropriate language for social media and texting purposes and more formal writing for academic rubrics (Wood, Kemp, & Plester, 2013). The revision process must have clear strategies that promote the expectations of the writing genre the student is learning.

Emerging research has proven automated essay scoring (AES) systems are reliable in giving valid feedback on the quality of student work on writing assessments (Shermis & Burstein, 2013). While these systems offer a clear evaluation of a student's learning after a unit of study, advances in the technology may be used to provide instructional support by testing student deficiencies and growth prior to and during learning (MacArthur, 2016). The author maintains further studies are needed to analyze how AES increases student performance.

Revision demands students be critical readers who are proficient in sentence and content comprehension, structure, connecting ideas to prior knowledge, and evaluating text with a focus on main ideas and organization, which bring challenges for struggling writers (MacArthur, 2016). The revision stage separates expert and novice writers, since proficient writers spend substantial time revising work to consider how audience and purpose align to the content, organization, and style of the final product (MacArthur, 2012). The authors contend expert writers use the revision stage to refine and readdress ideas aligned to the writing task in order to draft a more comprehensive and focused end product.

In addition, the revision stage can broaden a teacher's perspective into how to best guide students to address deficiencies that not only address problems in the writing task at hand, but help students overcome common mistakes in successive writing assignments (Alber, 2016; MacArthur, 2012). In essence, instructing students on effective revision strategies teaches techniques of evaluation, the consideration of audience and purpose, and methods to approach inadequacies while working through writing tasks (Alber, 2016; MacArthur, 2012). The struggling writer will learn how to self-regulate deficiencies in the revision phase, which will lead to a more calculated approach to addressing faults in thinking or applying sound principles in future writing endeavors.

TEACHERS AND PEER-TO-PEER REVISION STRATEGIES

Teachers who effectively model revision strategies enhance writing skills and self-regulation strategies in students, whether by guiding students through methods to evaluate the fundamentals of writing principles or taking part in student–teacher conferences where an analysis of these principles is practiced in real time while editing (Alber, 2016; Graham et al., 2012; Harris, Graham,

MacArthur, Reid, & Mason, 2011). Since revision has been proven to be an essential principle to writing and effective writing instruction, feedback and practical activities can be offered in multiple cycles where the struggling writer works at improving a piece of writing (MacArthur, 2016).

Students must be taught editing techniques while working independently and with peers during the revision process, since struggling writers can find teacher commentary to be enigmatic or choose to not use the commentary in ways that improve writing quality (Varner, Roscoe, & McNamara, 2013). Students working with partners or in groups to plan, draft, revise, and edit saw a 31 percentile-point increase in quality of writing (Graham & Harris, 2016).

Philippakos and MacArthur (2014) studied elementary school students who were assigned to different groups during the revision phase: reviewers, readers, and a control group. Using a rubric, reviewers were asked to rate and offer suggestions on how to improve six persuasive papers. Readers read the papers without an evaluation tool, and the control group was given narrative texts to read. All the students were asked to revise a pretest essay, then write and revise two subsequent essays. The study revealed students in the "reviewers" group produced higher-quality essays with more elements of persuasion.

Offering students practice reviewing and analyzing papers from anonymous peer authors trains students to give effective peer reviews (MacArthur, 2016). Having students learn revision strategies using anonymous papers has three advantages: this approach allows students to analyze multiple papers quickly; the teacher can offer frameworks for groups learning evaluation and revision strategies; and, finally, papers can be discreetly chosen to reveal problems and revision potential (MacArthur, 2016).

A study of fifth graders suggests students who were given time to read and discuss samples of a writing assignment achieved greater gains during the revision process (Moore & MacArthur, 2012). Students were broken down into three groups: one group of students read and discussed the samples, a second group of observers took notes and discussed a list of criteria the readers were expected to follow, and the third control group practiced writing. The readers in the study revised with a more distinguishable awareness of audience and better-discussed alternative perspectives than the control group. The authors (Moore & MacArthur, 2012) contend that analyzing samples using the think-aloud discussion strategy improved the students' awareness and attentiveness to audience.

While giving feedback in peer reviews (Cho & MacArthur, 2011; Crinon, 2012; Philippakos & MacArthur, 2016), students are gaining perspectives and seeing models of writing that increase learning. Research shows students who read or observe student-readers analyzing the effectiveness of text show marked improvement in writing quality (Moore & MacArthur, 2012).

GRAMMAR

Effective writing instruction parlays specific principles and writing strategies to address individual deficiencies. Meeting the needs of students is a challenge when deficiencies are widespread, which is often the case when teachers consider lessons on grammar. Although grammar is taught in most elementary classrooms, one common reason grammar is not taught extensively in older grades is due to levels of proficiency among students being too varied, making certain lessons rudimentary for advanced writers. Therefore, grammar instruction must be tallied and tailored to meet the needs of specific groups of students.

Designing a network for collaboration increases a student's time and engagement while doing revisions (Beach, Newell, & VanDerHeide, 2016) by allowing proficient students to enrich understanding of key concepts while working to assist students who struggle with specific principles. In addition to practicing grammar rules, searching for grammar flaws during the revision process can lead to a focused approach at looking how individual words build and support key points in a writing piece.

There are five categories to consider when developing grammar lessons: why grammar is essential to teach; when grammar lessons become appropriate; how lessons should be taught; what specific lessons will help; and who should be in charge of offering advice, feedback, and strategies (Hudson, 2016). Grammar is a tool that helps students develop methods to appropriately think through the writing process and how ideas connect to the rules of language (Hudson, 2016).

Addressing the question of "when" grammar should be taught, Hudson (2016) suggests there is a choice between having a system of teaching grammar that follows the expectations of a syllabus and developing grammar lessons as issues arise among students after the completion of writing tasks. When focusing on the "how," grammar tenets should be taught by rote memorization and by offering strategies that help students understand the fundamentals of language using grammar terminology and through diagramming sentences (Hudson, 2016).

When determining what grammar should be taught, Hudson (2016) suggests two approaches. The first is to teach before assigning a writing task to help students avoid common errors. The second is to address grammar concerns while analyzing a student's potential for growth in areas of deficiency. A practical method to address grammar needs is coming up with a formula to recognize problems most consistent in a group of students. While analyzing student work, the teacher must read with a focus on finding the most common grammar problems present in the largest number of students.

The teacher should design lessons that have students practice these grammar errors, and use the more proficient students to manage and support the struggling writers' attempts. An effective way to teach grammar is to pull a group of the class's five best writers to enrich personal understanding of concepts under study by assisting peers in revising assignments or working through samples with grammatical flaws. The enrichment students become the managers and support systems within groups, and, in doing so, reinforce understanding of key grammar concepts.

A lack of rigor in grammar lessons in recent decades has produced a generation of teachers that is not fully equipped to teach the nuances of language rules (Hudson, 2016), so enabling students to understand and teach each other the basic rules that relate to the parts of speech and common errors is an approach that will reinforce the concepts and facilitate ownership in learning.

STRATEGIES

Students who do not plan before attempting a writing task use the revision stage as a strategy to evaluate and pinpoint ideas that can be addressed and refined in later drafts (MacArthur, 2016). Kiuhara et al. (2012) tested a group of tenth graders with disabilities after teaching the AIMS planning tool, and found use of the strategy helped students offer better context in introductions. In addition, students who used AIMS spent more time planning higher-quality essays that had more elaboration, background information, and more varied perspectives.

Like many prewriting tools, AIMS can be implemented as an effective rubric or discussion point during peer-to-peer edits or student–teacher conferences. Students can gain insight into how to better attract the audience's attention (A), identify the problem for the reader to understand the issue (I), map the problem under discussion as it develops throughout a writing task (M), then state the thesis more succinctly as clarification is needed (S).

Students also benefited from strategies with methods for revising ideas (Song & Ferretti, 2013), evaluating standards and further improving essays. Song and Ferretti (2013) reviewed an SRSD strategy to teach argumentative writing using the Ask and Answer Critical Question (ASCQ) technique. When using this tool, students answer questions about the consequences and examples that offer support in the overall argument.

Song and Feretti (2013) found students using this strategy needed fewer revisions to address counterarguments, viewpoints, or support to refute evidence from the opposing side. While evaluating argumentative writing instructional techniques in college, students who were taught specific critical questioning techniques wrote higher-quality essays that incorporated more counterarguments, perspectives, and a stronger refutation of ideas (Song & Ferretti, 2013). As a practical application, these questioning techniques could be applied to revision workshops and discussions that guide the struggling writer to offer more comprehensive support in argumentative writing tasks.

Another method to help the struggling writer align valid support to meet the criteria of writing assignments is using the C-D-O Strategy, which is outlined here:

Compare (search for areas where the text does not go in line with its intended meaning)
Diagnose (identify reasons for any discrepancies)
Operate (revise and evaluate revision that ties the text to its intended meaning)

Students can approach the C-D-O strategy during two focused edits: the first by working with individual sentences in a draft; the second by using the strategy to analyze and align paragraphs in a subsequent revision. This strategy enables struggling writers to self-regulate through a structured format that searches for writing problems (Troia 2014).

APPLIED PRACTICES

Show, Don't Tell

A writing principle taught in school is "show, don't tell," which asks students to be visually specific when describing objects or situations in a writing assignment. However, the struggling writer is limited by this burden: the student cannot show what the student doesn't know. In short, the student with little knowledge of subjects can only offer banal responses.

Learning to self-regulate writing means teaching strategies to overcome moments when the student writes in generalities, which is why offering students topics of high interest and relevance is a sound practice when designing writing lessons (Bazerman, 2016). Guiding students through research is one way to approach the challenge of students not knowing content well enough to write proficiently. An example would be to open a class by asking students to write a paragraph about a subject that is likely unfamiliar.

For this example, the subject will be the civil rights movement. After students struggle to come up with specific words and ideas related to the movement, the teacher offers notes on a PowerPoint presentation that includes images, video clips, and excerpts from speeches that defined the struggle. With notes in hand, students are tasked with rewriting the assignment, but this time by offering specific moments that occurred during the civil rights movement. A final assignment would be for students to reflect on the first and second paragraphs, and how research specifically guided students to describe and define the writing task.

Since writing is a reflection of a student's knowledge of a subject matter, enrichment exercises can be built around this concept. Students could be given homework or extra credit when offering recaps on a documentary watched at home, or an interesting quote that was read or heard. The struggling writer should be taught and reminded that the expansion of knowledge and life experience works to the writer's advantage. This builds confident and well-rounded writers over time.

Specificity

Since the revision stage is when the struggling writer takes ownership of deficiencies in a draft (and as a writer), the more hours the struggling writer spends analyzing work in the revision phase, the more proficient first drafts will become.

The first principle to revising is learning through application that specific words are always better than vague words. In all stages of thinking and writing, students must be reminded that word choice must be concise and clear enough to have the reader imagine an idea or scene as the writer intends. In other words, if it's up for interpretation, it's the job of the writer to interpret the idea for the reader to experience as the writer wishes.

There is a simple formula that illustrates this point: Give readers an experience = opening readers' minds and memories = emotional connections. The writer who follows this formula to get the reader emotionally connected will have an audience that is more eager to continue reading, whether because the reader is entertained or simply finds the information intriguing.

Analyzing word choice in the revision process will help students respect and manage how words and sentences unravel and connect to central ideas. Whether seasoned or new, a writer's first thought is usually common, if not outright cliché. Therefore, if 100 students were asked to describe school, the same words would come up time and again: boring, too much work, a place of discovery, concerned teachers, mean teachers, bullying, homework, tests. The struggling writer must learn to look at word choice with that principled understanding in mind, and then use strategies to craft writing that builds on a personal style of presenting ideas in a unique fashion.

A key to engaging struggling writers with the show, don't tell writing principle is offering prompts that help students write on a deeper level. Writing on topics that are familiar—relationships, pets, common fears, pop culture trends—will enhance learning (Bazerman, 2016). So the show, don't tell principle must be taught with writing prompts that tap into the struggling writer's expertise. This is how the struggling writer will be guided to gain confidence in building distinct and original words, sentences, and paragraphs.

An exercise to build understanding of this principle is to offer students an opportunity to write letters to friends, family members, or notable acquaintances. After a first draft, the student approaches a rewrite by looking for moments that offer general descriptions, then drawing on the student's deeper knowledge of the subject to give specific "shows." For example, if the student describes a friend as "funny," "reliable," or "loving," the student should be guided to expand these descriptions into specific moments that animate this person fitting into these descriptions

Doing this with topics that are emotionally relevant to the struggling writer will increase engagement. Better, the struggling writer will take more ownership in perfecting this principle since the letter is a source of pride and written with a practical purpose in mind.

Letter writing can be used to issue complaints as well, whether in a business transaction or customer service experience that left the student feeling offended. The same process would be applied: write a first draft, then search for moments ("rude," "unhelpful," "disinterested") where the student could have specifically "shown" these characteristics happening during the experience.

Offering students sentences with vague details also encourages and builds confidence in mastering the principle of "show, don't tell." For example, a sentence as simple as "The girl is mean" would offer students an opportunity to be more specific with "girl" and "mean" to help the reader experience both. In time, the struggling writer will discover when words and ideas are up for interpretation, and how to become more proficient at interpreting each for the reader.

Appraising the Value of Words

Editing is the writer's attempt at judging the clarity, originality, and credibility of a piece of writing. Clarity can be gained and refined with a clear understanding of the parts of speech. Since an analysis of word choice is the most simplified measurement to improve writing, having a focused edit on the parts of speech will set the standard, particularly when looking for areas where the text does not align to intended meaning (Troia, 2014).

Exercises that guide the struggling writer to identify and improve word choice will build confidence in understanding the building blocks that make up effective writing. One practice would be to have students seek out action verbs in a piece of writing, circling each, then offering a synonym or two in the margin that might better fit the personality of the subject. This activity gets the struggling writer focused on enhancing verbs to maximize cohesion and engagement in writing.

Another technique is to give students sentences with strong verbs to identify and explain what makes each effective, then to come up with synonyms that would heighten the intended effect of weaker examples. Practicing this exercise in sentences as a class or in groups will guide the student with learning disabilities to practice this approach while editing a piece of writing.

While word processing, teachers can guide students to right-click verbs (or other word choices) and search for synonyms that might better fit the personality of the subject or idea being described. Websites such as www.thesaurus. com have the same effect, and offer students a resource to more calculated expression. While working through these applied practices, the struggling writer learns to weigh the value of words, which leads to more precise and credible writing.

Exercises that enable students to work through adjective and adverb choices help the struggling writer recognize how descriptive words must be used with a succinct purpose. Since struggling writers often use adjectives and adverbs as redundancies (he smiled happily, the angry teacher yelled), teaching these simple parts of speech will help students learn the economy of words, and how each word should be used with precision.

Following the format of the previous verb exercises, activities engaging students in the use of adjectives and adverbs promote a writing principle that makes writing more fluid and concise: the adjective or adverb must be 100 percent essential to further a point that would not be fully understood by the reader without the adjective or adverb to clarify the point.

Whether through assessing the parts of speech or circling each to weigh the deeper purpose, strategies that have the struggling writer address word choice will foster confidence and a deeper understanding of the nuances of language. This approach, using a single word, can enhance a student's willingness to engage in the deeper themes present in a writing task.

Celebrations

A principle to proficient writing is recognizing when brainstorming, the generation of ideas, or the writing process itself was effectively fulfilled within a writing task. Activities that allow the struggling writer to search for and celebrate these moments—whether a word choice, a rhetorical device, or an idea—enable students to begin recognizing areas in writing that did not meet the standard of great writing.

Students should be given time to go back and reflect on previous writing assignments, or to write a journal entry and take a moment to write a short reflection on a masterful writing moment. In time, the student can then be given a secondary task of seeking moments that don't work, and methods to address areas of weakness to improve the overall quality.

As students search for moments that fulfill the standards of great writing, a reflection phase is essential to helping the struggling writing decipher the thought process that led to effective writing. In essence, every word and sentence and paragraph should be rewritten until each follows the same model of great writing.

This practice can be applied while reading. Struggling writers must be taught strategies to better understand what is consciously happening while reading, so the student may be better equipped to manipulate and explore words and ideas in a similar fashion. This is called "reading like a writer."

Offer students a passage with vivid imagery that is relatable to adolescence or young adulthood, then ask students to find the most interesting language choices in the passage and how these words and ideas tie into what the student knows about the world based on personal experience. This writing principle reinforces why brainstorming is vital, as well as why it's essential to leave a space underneath graphic organizers to list research points that need to be explored.

Critiques

The critique gives the writer a chance to gain perspective from a reader to see how well ideas and support of those ideas are understood. This is essential, since everybody reads differently and has different styles of communicating and different abilities to understand. The critique helps the struggling writer step outside his or her writing to see how a peer interprets it. Because of this, it's essential for students to not take critiques personally, so certain expectations should be instituted to guide in the process. The purpose of receiving a critique should never result in a feeling of judgment but should be regarded as an opportunity to gain wisdom from another perspective on how work can be improved.

Helping struggling writers find value in receiving critiques from peers will foster accelerated growth in writing proficiency. Since writing is often a source of insecurity for individuals with LLD, asking for critiques can become a source of stress for students. Pairing a student with a trusted and valuable partner to critique work can raise engagement and increase a student's willingness to work on revisions (Beach, Newell, & VanDerHeide, 2016).

There are basic areas that can be covered in a critique: areas that lacked specificity, areas where the writing became boring, and areas where there was confusion. As always, celebrating areas of strengths will give the struggling writer confidence, and become models for how weaker portions of writing should be approached.

FINAL THOUGHTS

The editing and revision stages of the writing process must be stressed as opportunities for the struggling writer to recognize, control, and self-regulate deficiencies in the writing process. Since the educator must work with any number of writing deficits among a group of fledgling writers, the editing and revision processes should aim to streamline learning by urging students to take ownership in surmounting personal deficiencies in the writing process.

Essentially, this is the stage where the struggling writer diagnoses weaknesses, such as word choice, staying on topic, and searching for consistent grammar flaws. After learning how to recognize inadequacies, the struggling writer can begin to prescribe personal methods of fixing each during the commission of writing or within the revision process. Focused edits, like using the C-D-O strategy to scan for inconsistencies in textual meaning and support, can then be applied to self-regulate writing.

A teacher's red marks become an archaic form of feedback when the struggling writer is guided to search and remediate flawed approaches throughout the writing process. Of course, students must edit work that has been written with best efforts; otherwise, the prescribed methods for fixing deficiencies will be founded in baseless half attempts. This mindset helps the struggling writer put more passion and purpose into writing assignments, which cycles forward into proficiency while editing and revising.

In time, automated technologies that assess writing competencies will merge with the editing and revision stages. Until then, struggling writers should be guided to revise in repeated cycles. The student begins by attempting a writing task alone without any instruction. A writing principle is then taught where the student must evaluate, identify, and revise deficiencies that were not known before this instruction.

The student then completes a rewrite by fixing any areas of needed improvement. Finally, the student reflects on specific moments in the first and second drafts that reveal the student recognizes deficiencies and needed remediation to address each. With this, the student begins to collect portfolio artifacts proving mastery of various writing principles, and, better, how to recognize, control, and self-regulate common deficiencies

POINTS TO REMEMBER

- *Teacher feedback, peer reviews, instruction in goals and strategies, offering students evaluation criteria, and enabling students to observe readers evaluating text all increase competency in revision and overall writing quality.*

- *This generation of students is faced with having to learn to differentiate between appropriate language for social media and texting purposes and more formal writing for academic rubrics.*
- *Revision demands students be critical readers who are proficient in sentence and content comprehension, structure, connecting ideas to prior knowledge, and evaluating text with a focus on main ideas and organization, which bring challenges for struggling writers.*
- *Students must be taught editing techniques while working independently and with peers during the revision process, since struggling writers can find teacher commentary to be enigmatic or choose to not use the commentary in ways that improve writing quality.*
- *There are five categories to consider when developing grammar lessons, namely, why grammar is essential to teach; when grammar lessons become appropriate; how lessons should be taught; what specific lessons will help; and who should be in charge of offering advice, feedback, and strategies.*
- *While evaluating argumentative writing instructional techniques in college, students who were taught specific critical questioning techniques wrote higher-quality essays that incorporated more counterarguments, perspectives, and a stronger refutation of ideas.*

Chapter 9

The Promise of Writer's Workshop: Practical Approaches to Engage all Students

The writing workshop accelerates learning based on the sharing of ideas, a centered focus on audience and purpose, and tracing measurements of growth over time to help the struggling writer see faults in writing and thinking while interpreting and revising writing tasks in teams (Crinon, 2012). Students show gains in learning and a willingness to explore new ideas when presented with critiques and conversations from peers offering differing viewpoints (Beach, Newell, & VanDerHeide, 2016).

The writing workshop model also takes the burden off teachers having to be the exclusive stalwarts to learning, which results in a more efficient means to build confidence and development in the struggling writer.

Collaborative writing occurs when there is no competition among students, but, rather, when expectations follow a sociocultural perspective where common goals and tools are used with a sense of shared responsibility and equal accountability (Mercer & Howe, 2012). With today's technology, teachers can facilitate and manage collaborative writing by using blogs and Google Docs as digital tools for students to share and critique work (Thompson, 2012).

Collaborative writing allows students to offer personal problem-solving techniques, strategies for planning and revising, and a more fluid methodology to work through the writing process itself; giving feedback to peers helps the struggling writer reflect on approaches and thought processes that occur while writing for distinct audiences and purposes (Crinon, 2012).

Offering individualized feedback based on teacher commentary may take days or weeks, while peer-to-peer feedback can be extensive and instantaneous inside the writing workshop model (MacArthur, 2016). During collaborative feedback, students benefit from seeing and receiving critical analysis of work; thus, the process requires a give and take between students (MacArthur, 2016). Still, there is potential for students to lack the capacity to teach strategies and concepts in the workshop model, or for dissension to occur when offering critiques or accepting criticism from peers.

The writing workshop model using collaboration activities is not used in many classrooms (Lacina & Collins Block, 2012). When designed effectively, collaborative writing lessons and activities have potential to increase confidence in the struggling writer learning to incorporate various perspectives, though more research is still needed to qualify collaboration's relationship to self-efficacy (Bruning & Kauffman, 2016).

SETTING UP WORKSHOPS

When designing a writing workshop model, the teacher must consider modified methods to maximize practice and engagement activities to circumvent common challenges that occur during peer-to-peer discussions and critiques. In this way, the workshop model must be refined during and after sessions by students and teachers designing more streamlined methods for learning. Once calibrated to enhance collaboration, the writing workshop adds momentum and targeted practice that guides the struggling writer to succeed with increasing confidence.

Collaboration that goes beyond traditional writing genres assessed by teachers helps the development of struggling writers (Bazerman, 2016). While offering strategies for critiques during writing workshops, students benefit from watching teachers model thought processes that lay out standards of evaluation (MacArthur, 2016). Students are more likely to edit after receiving peer-to-peer feedback that promotes collaboration as a way to discuss the complexity of writing (Beach, Newell, & VanDerHeide, 2016).

Teachers must have a firm grasp on interpreting and using assessments to drive instruction (Stahl & McKenna, 2012) that can build strategies for writing workshop models. When developing anchor sets to guide talking points in writing workshops, teachers must choose text based on three criteria: quantitative measures based on lexiles; qualitative data based on benchmark texts; a consideration of the reader and what is expected during the reading (Hiebert, 2012).

In short, the anchor sets must be accessible to a student's reading ability, go in line with standards needed to evaluate a final product, and be offered using activities the student can effectively work through to understand the standards being met.

It is beneficial to use contrasting samples that reflect work meeting standards under discussion with work that falls short of expectations (Troia, 2014). Discussion points should focus on one or two standards represented in the samples, such as word choice, fluency or structure—one text may illustrate vivid imagery and fluency, while the second has instances of clichés or vague language choices (Troia, 2014).

Using anonymous papers to practice evaluation and revision strategies allows students to see a variety of papers focused on specific processes and problems that are common among struggling writers (MacArthur, 2016). Moore and MacArthur (2012) found students who evaluated argumentative essays based on discussions focused on questioning revised higher-quality essays with more varied perspectives. Discussing and modeling best practices in the writing workshop model follows the principle of considering alternative standpoints to rewrite a final product that meets the standards of proficiency.

ADVICE ON GROUPING

The writing workshop may be hindered when a student is not able to decipher the fundamentals of effective reading and language analysis. Whether a writer has deficiencies in understanding vocabulary, structural nuances, or symbolic wordplay represented in rhetorical devices, the end result may be a team member who is ill-equipped to offer sound advice while analyzing a peer's work.

Pairing or grouping students without disabilities to offer strategies that help struggling peers engage and interact with the learning environment is cited as an evidence-based practice (Fettig, 2013). There are four language systems that make up an evidence-based conceptual model of writing systems in the brain, namely, language by ear, language by mouth, language by eye, language by hand (Berninger, 2015; Berninger & Niedo, 2014).

An effective writing workshop should seek to group students based on the development level of like language systems to have more integrated interaction during activities. As an applied practice, having a variety of exercises (such as think-aloud sessions, presentations, or note taking) will help teachers team students in groups with like-minded learners, or with learners who can model standards from an alternate perspective.

An analysis of successful writers revealed the standard of high-quality writing must take into account different profiles of writing styles that can be deemed proficient (Crossley, Roscoe, & McNamara, 2014). One of these included the "action and depiction style," where the writing had a bigger emphasis on action through verbs and descriptive wording. Another was "academic style," where the writer showed a propensity for structure and complex sentences. In this way, the authors suggested writers must be judged based on developing differently, so consideration of style is paramount in managing writing workshop or assessment formulas.

The Response to Intervention (RTI) framework offers a multitiered approach for teachers to consider methods and interventions to assist struggling students, with the most intensive approach coming in Tier 3, where learning is typically gained in small groups or during one-on-one settings (Cusumano, Algozzine, & Algozzine, 2014). This system usually includes screening, monitoring, and data analysis to decide on the best approach to learning (Deshler & Cornett, 2012). The role of the teacher must remain fluid—assisting Tier 3 students in one-on-one conferences, and rotating students to work together as problems or potential solutions arise during the implementation of the writing workshop.

Allowing students to reflect on collaboration efforts can help teachers identify strategies and approaches when peers work effectively, or when collaborative group members contest alternative perspectives and suggestions being offered during activities (Duffy, 2014). As an applied practice, students can rate group members' performance, or the effectiveness of the group as a whole, with suggestions on how to apply some variance of strategies in future sessions.

APPLIED PRACTICE

There are typically four levels of writers a teacher must identify and manage while designing an effective writing workshop model. Though individual learning styles are not taken into account here, categorizing proficiency and engagement among writers leads to more effective grouping to facilitate growth in the struggling writer working through the writing workshop model.

- The lowest level—writers who fall under this category want to get writing assignments done with minimal effort due to a lack of confidence or understanding of writing fundamentals. These writers are capable of learning, but without a foundation of success while writing, become fearful of trying.
- The mid-low level—these are the writers who have a basic understanding of some writing fundamentals, but lack the focus or discipline to refine strengths, resulting in unnecessary mistakes.
- The low-high level—these are writers with a strong foundation of the writing fundamentals, but are careless or write in moments of distraction, which keeps these writers from meeting standards on the highest level.
- The highest level—these writers struggle because most assignments do not offer challenges to go deeper into the writing process.

When pairing students, the highest-level writers can be teamed up with any group to reinforce knowledge of the writing process, along with strategies writers must use to generate and move ideas. The lowest-level student is best paired with the low-high-level writer. This increases awareness and focus in the low-high-level writer who seeks to help the lowest-level writer take ownership of the strategies or standards of proficient writing. The mid-low-level student can also see gains by helping the lowest-level writers, but the writing workshop must have specific criteria for analysis and discussion.

The writing workshop enables and engages students to direct a deeper focus to writing strategies and standards under study because the process is social, rather than an individual effort done in silence to meet the expectations of a teacher or assessment. The writing workshop employs a wider scope of thinking, since the struggling writer will know finished work will be read, analyzed, and critiqued by peers. All of this heightens the writer's awareness of audiences when working through writing tasks.

READING

Since students read on varying levels, assigning groups to facilitate a writing workshop model must take into account focused strategies that are attainable for all learners. The teacher should model the expectations, then group students according to learning styles and abilities to work through specific writing tasks and standards. Students need instruction that systematically lays out clear objectives while learning how to read proficiently (Beck & Beck, 2012; Smartt, & Glaser, 2010). This approach will guide students to read with a purposeful focus when offering critiques in the writing workshop.

Writing workshops that allow students to analyze argumentative writing have advantages. Reading argumentative essays widens students' exposure to alternative perspectives while considering rhetorical choices to express viewpoints (Warren, 2013). This guides the struggling writer to help audiences understand how evidence supports claims made in argumentative points (De La Paz, Ferretti, Wissinger, Yee, & MacArthur, 2012). Students who were offered opportunities to read and discuss persuasiveness in samples of work spent more time revising final drafts that produced drafts with better quality and more evidence of audience awareness (Moore & MacArthur, 2012).

Students who have a clear understanding of author's perspectives are better able to summarize the legitimacy and cohesiveness of those perspectives while writing (Warren, 2013).

The writing workshop allows students to see varying perspectives and develop a better understanding of differing perspectives. Applying this workshop model prior to the completion of a writing task has the same effect; the struggling writer is able to team up with peers who help brainstorm and plan broader support of key points that can be developed while writing.

Students who are guided to seek out alternative perspectives during critiques are more apt to cite varying perspectives or qualify their points when writing (Beach, Newell, & VanDerHeide, 2016). High-level college students were more prone to offer better proof to qualify an audience's awareness of differing perspectives (Aull & Lancaster, 2014). While critiquing during a writing workshop, students see how other writers use evidence to support claims by adopting an audience's perspective (De La Paz et al., 2012).

APPLIED PRACTICE: PORTFOLIOS

Since revision is agreed to promote growth and foster understanding during writing workshops and writing instruction, offering multiple cycles of revision with feedback can improve student writing (MacArthur, 2016). Keeping running drafts in a portfolio allows the struggling writer to reflect on thinking in the early stages of the writing process, then recognize best practices that were followed to fulfill the expectations of writing tasks.

Portfolios are invaluable to help the struggling writer reflect on specific writing principles learned over time. The key to the portfolio is not the submitted drafts so much as a clear and consistent reflection on the evolution of concepts learned. Having students revisit old assignments and analyze deficiencies (even months after the assignment, but when new principles of writing have been practiced and learned) is proof the struggling writer has mastered the necessary principles to be considered proficient.

This point needs to be emphasized: the portfolio is most effective when there is a component of deep reflection on specific concepts learned. Typically, the portfolio shows the student reacting to teacher commentary without reflecting on how teacher or peer commentary helped the student align thinking to broader principles. When this happens, the student turns in a rough draft, and is given commentary on a variety of issues, from grammar to organization and specificity. The student rewrites the essay fixing some or all of these comments, but the final product does not show any mastery of a specific skill other than reacting to a deficiency based on commentary from a teacher or peer. In short, the struggling writer patches up a series of problems without revealing or qualifying a deeper understanding of specific principles.

The portfolio must be designed around individual, focused writing principles and methods. This will increase engagement by having students go beyond simple compliance. For example, if the student shows a deficiency in understanding why it's essential to activate prior knowledge, a teacher marking students' assignments with comments about grammar and structure is counterproductive and may make the student feel overwhelmed.

The student must, instead, be guided to generate more brainstorming charts, then streamline these strategies into the writing process during a rewrite of the assignment. This shows students how brainstorming enables thinking about a writing situation beforehand, and, more importantly, how that technique lends itself to the writing process. A reflection of this strategy after the assignment should be designed to summarize a student's deeper understanding of the principle.

The writing workshop model and subsequent portfolio entries must offer students quality time to discuss, on an individualized level, how using that technique simplified the writing process. An effective method here is asking the struggling writer to reflect on how not using the technique would have made the process more difficult. At year's end, the portfolio must offer a progression of work samples that sought to enable students to take ownership while discussing what works and doesn't work while working through the principles of effective writing.

FINAL THOUGHTS

Writer's Workshop leads to gains in proficiency when students recognize writing tasks can be completed using a variety of approaches developed by differing vantage points. Students reading multiple essays crafted by peers will see writing as a fluid, evolving process of generating ideas, then refining each to fulfill the expectations of the assignment. Better, the writing workshop can offer feedback in a timely manner, which aids the student's ability to more accurately study the thinking processes that lead to proficiency while writing in the moment.

In other words, peer collaboration can happen moments after a writing assignment is completed, whereas receiving commentary or other feedback from a teacher may take days, if not weeks. By that time, the struggling writer must strain to remember the thought processes that developed writing in the first place. Knowing a peer critique is imminent encourages the struggling writer to focus more on meeting the expectations of the writing task, especially those related to an understanding of audience.

Writing is an intimate and personal exploration of thoughts and opinions, so the struggling writer may first have to overcome feelings of inadequacy that limit free expression; thus, recognizing and celebrating each writer's strengths must be a consistent expectation during the writing workshop. No matter how broken grammar may be, or how basic word choice or proofs may come across, there is a writing moment in a piece that shines above the rest. Having students always celebrate great writing moments will lead to higher self-efficacy in the drafting and revision stages.

Students can be given guided instruction on what to search for and improve, which can help the struggling writer practice heightening awareness of grammar flaws, organizational snafus, or developing better proofs and perspectives. As stated in previous chapters, students are more apt to self-regulate the writing process after learning to recognize and take ownership of specific writing principles. The writing workshop becomes the most expedient method to allow students needed practice of evaluating and refining writing principles.

Designing a workshop is not easy—educators must consider students' learning approaches, reading proficiencies, and willingness to participate. In this way, the writing workshop becomes a fluid activity—much like the writing process itself—where the educator and students have open discussions on what's working and what might work better next time.

The goal of the writing workshop is to share and enhance perspectives within a writing task; thus, writing workshop groups that don't blend well as teams will still find gains by modeling this approach of deconstructing and cultivating sound writing principles.

POINTS TO REMEMBER

- *Collaborative writing occurs when common goals and tools are used with a sense of shared responsibility and equal accountability.*
- *Collaborative writing allows students to offer personal problem-solving techniques, strategies for planning and revising, and a more fluid methodology to work through the writing process itself.*
- *Offering individualized feedback based on teacher commentary may take days or weeks, while peer-to-peer feedback can be extensive and instantaneous inside the writing workshop model.*
- *Students are more likely to edit after receiving peer-to-peer feedback that promotes collaboration as a way to discuss the complexity of writing.*
- *An evidence-based practice includes pairing or grouping students without disabilities to offer strategies that help struggling peers engage and interact with the learning environment.*
- *Reading argumentative essays widens students' exposure to alternative perspectives while considering rhetorical choices to express viewpoints.*
- *Allowing students to reflect on collaboration efforts can help teachers identify strategies and approaches when peers work effectively, or when collaborative group members contest alternative perspectives and suggestions being offered during activities.*

Chapter 10

Technology as a Tool to Improve Writing: I-phones to Laptops

Advances in technology will dictate shifts in educating learning disabled and or struggling students who once had to rely exclusively on teachers for instruction and support. Online tutorials, forums, speech-to-text programs, and advancing word processing all function to help map, organize, and generate information for the struggling writer. This will result in a sea change in how to address deficiencies in language learning. Since students are often more proficient at using technology than teachers, the struggling writer would feel empowered in a more digitalized learning environment where students take ownership in designing and formatting lessons for teachers to offer instruction on the principles of sound writing.

Recent data reveals nearly three in four students in the United States are writing below proficient levels (National Center for Education Statistics, 2012), so embracing new technologies to complement student writing outside the classroom seems to be an area where the struggling writer can receive needed practice and a reinforcement of sound principles.

Since college students reported that text messaging, emailing, and sharing lecture notes online were used for social purposes and to maintain social relationships, designing lessons that incorporate writing principles within these genres are a practical solution for the struggling writer to practice and model what is learned in school with common communication outside the classroom (Pigg et al., 2014). This, in turn, can help the student to incorporate writing not as homework, but as enrichment exercises completed in the commission of social media, texts, and other online communications.

Though traditional essay and argumentative writing instruction remain common writing disciplines taught in most classrooms, the changing times demand an expansion of practical writing genres that maximize student engagement in best practices while working in the classroom and beyond.

Writing principles remain the same across genres, so a focus on developing lessons and strategies using technological resources will not only help the struggling writer use more tools but streamline the approach to teaching writing as a utility function in both real life and academia.

EASE OF USE

The technology age brings solutions and challenges when implementing strategies in the classroom. Some students have technology readily available and are apt to use it, while others have fewer resources and see technology as a hindrance to thinking and learning. Since school districts are increasing technological resources such as computers and high-speed Internet, and with the workplace demanding a proficiency in being able to use technology to complete day-to-day tasks, students who are not savvy with technological resources must be given an outlet to learn and practice learning using modern approaches.

While learning to write, students who struggle with handwriting, typing, or spelling can suffer a disconnect while transcribing ideas onto the page and screen (Graham & Harris, 2016); thus, using the most fluid approach for individual students is the preferred method. Since state assessments are predominantly performed by word processing, students who handwrite during strategy sessions or practice tests may also be at a disadvantage. The struggling writer who is a poor typist should be given the opportunity to handwrite initial drafts, and then transcribe the text using a word processor to model the testing expectations.

To increase competence in typing, instruction and practice time should be dedicated to increase proficiency with keyboarding or using other available technological resources. When typing, writing occurs in sequences, or bursts of activity, when the writer produces words before distinct pauses to think further about the writing task or process what was just written (Torrance, 2016).

The burst lengths are shorter depending on age, ability to type, or language impairments (Alves, Branco, Castro, & Olive, 2012; Connelly, Dockrell, Walter, & Critten, 2012). This illustrates the need to offer struggling writers courses, or at least time to practice, using word processors to improve performance when this format is demanded on assessments or class expectations.

Enabling the struggling writer with technology such as word processors and the Internet offers advantages over traditional pencil and paper writing: text can be cut, copied, deleted, added, or rewritten with a few keystrokes; the presentation is legible to all readers and can be spellchecked and shared using blogs or forums; the Internet also enables students to gather information to generate ideas and offer support (Graham & Harris, 2016).

Word processing enables the struggling writer to more easily transcribe and revise, streamline collaboration during different stages of the writing process, and share work on a global scale using the Internet (Troia, 2014). Computers, tablets, and cell phones with word processing capabilities must be used to teach students how to plan, write, revise, and publish work beginning in the early grades (Troia, 2014).

ONLINE FORUMS

Using online forums to teach the principles of writing engages students by incorporating the craft as a skill that can be used and refined outside the classroom. Since students are likely sending, receiving, and reading messages using social media, texting, and emails, offering writing instruction and practice in relation to these mediums will enable the struggling writer to understand the principles of writing in a practical way that applies directly to the student's social and academic experiences.

Online communication offers students a comfortable and familiar forum to write, collaborate, and share strategies with each other in all stages of writing. Zawilinski (2012) found first and fifth graders who communicated with one another on a blog developed new literacies, and were more eager to offer instructional strategies of these literacies to peers and teachers.

Since traditional writing genres remain the focus of education, further research must be done into writing instruction that focuses on the needs of a wider audience, such as is found in online written communication (Leu et al., 2016). Modern students are not writing for a wide readership, but for a teacher, classmate, or unknown assessor, and, as such, this may create a disconnect in how writing is applied to life outside school, making the struggling writer disengage when writing principles are not practiced (Leu et al., 2016).

Leu et al. (2016) say Internet communication focuses on the reader, receiver, or audience, so emphasizing audience in writing lessons will help the struggling writer gain context. Incorporating safe communication technologies have the potential to promote a dialogue for students to gain a deeper understanding on the importance of community and knowledge when writing to various audiences. In short, the struggling writer will be more apt to pay attention to a writing assignment where a more dynamic readership may be interpreting word choice, support, and varying perspectives.

Communication with global audiences outside the classroom is available using blogs, forums, message boards, and digital story platforms (Erstad, 2013; Purcell et al., 2013). Offering assignments for audiences beyond the classroom fosters development in understanding the social dimensions that take place when writing for wide audiences compared to school-based writing expectations (Beach, Newell, & VanDerHeide, 2016). This reinforces that writing principles for online communication along with the standards taught in the classroom must merge to assist the struggling writer's efforts in both realms.

PORTFOLIOS

The traditional portfolio showcasing artifacts written using traditional pencil and paper is becoming obsolete with emerging technology. These hardcopy portfolios often take up too much space, lack organization, can be incomplete, messy, or be lost during a unit of study. The modern age demands students begin developing electronic portfolios (e-portfolios) in lower grades to organize and trace the development of proficiencies in writing that is carried on throughout schooling.

E-portfolios can track the development of certain types of writing based on activities that foster social practices (Wills & Rice, 2013). At the University of Central Florida, researchers are analyzing e-portfolios of students to look for correlations and evidence of growth in writing across students' course loads (Wardle & Roozen, 2012). In time, technology should be able to diagnose areas of proficiency and give practical solutions for areas of deficiency in the struggling writer.

Using e-portfolios, technology can help the struggling writer trace self-efficacy during a writing task, namely, how personal confidence, interest, and expectations during the commission of a writing assignment either supported or diminished initial drafts evolving into final drafts (Bruning & Kauffman, 2016). In addition, technologies that coach, model, or showcase other students' work can also be studied to determine whether these platforms increased confidence in the struggling writer (Roscoe & McNamara, 2013).

Audience and writing purposes are expanding due to digital composition tools that incorporate genres, modes, language, and platforms (Schultz, Hull, & Higgs, 2016). The authors assert that this, along with an expansion of education into a multitude of arenas—public, private, international, informal—has further magnified the evolution of writing for varying needs.

Streamlining lessons using e-portfolios allows the struggling writer to not only determine needed areas of growth in various writing genres but gives organized, clear artifacts that allow the student to model and build on areas of proficiency with confidence. Using samples of work that effectively followed the expectations of a writing task, strategy, or rubric, the struggling writer is able to replicate, collaborate, and reflect on sound principles of writing over time.

APPLIED PRACTICE

Blogging. Offering the struggling writer a forum, such as a blog, to publish work has several advantages. First, publishing tools allow the student to see work posted beside peers, which may make the student more apt to read and analyze the work of others. Second, posting work to a blog allows the student to see writing as a practical skill to promote ideas in a global, real-world context. Finally, blogs give the student a clean format to access old writings to reflect on writing principles that are learned over time.

The process and principles of writing should be taught using topics that are of high interest so students understand the writing situation (Ferretti & Fan, 2016). This will lead to students being more confident and engaged while working through expectations of writing tasks. The goal is for the student to feel comfortable having work being published for consumption and critiques by peers, which will entice the struggling writer to revise more (Beach, Newell, & VanDerHeide, 2016), or to peruse and analyze similar work produced by others on the blog.

In time, short response and analysis essays examining literature, historical trends, or scientific theories can be published across curricula. This approach archives samples of writing the student can study or share with peers. In other words, the student who is posting summaries of historical trends (say the Battle of Gettysburg) will be more apt to read summaries from peers covering the Civil War and, ideally, be open to suggestions on how students present facts surrounding important events.

Once instituted, work that is published online can be accessed anywhere an Internet connection is available, which saves time and any space that was taken to store the traditional hardcopy portfolio method of learning. This helps the struggling writer revisit old work with ease and to critique and revise work as more fundamentals and knowledge is gained over time.

Students today must approach writing from a mass audience perspective. The old way of only having a teacher or peer read an essay draft is not preparing students for the world they engage in—social media, mass texts, and emailing, to name a few. Blogging will encourage a more focused approach to learning the principles of writing to not only inform and entertain, but to impress global audiences.

Online Visualization. The Internet is growing exponentially with content that can engage and enhance brainstorming and visualization when writing. From videos and documentaries to photographs and political cartoons, the potential for knowledge and reference points to guide the struggling writer is growing by the day.

One method that can be taught to encourage the struggling writer to be more specific with language choices is to offer students an opportunity to "borrow" from images or videos online that reflect a scene or idea the student is expected to describe. For example, while teaching the struggling writer methods to develop an intriguing setting, students can be guided to use Google Images to search for photographs that help the writer visualize the scene.

Whether it's a dark alley, blood-orange sunset, sporting event, or weather pattern, the struggling writer can click through photographs and videos to inspire an idea that lends itself to a vivid choice of words. This can also be done in history classes, when students use images of current events or photographs and paintings from events of the distant past to promote a deeper understanding of the subjects being taught.

FINAL THOUGHTS

The writing models outlined in this chapter are designed to help the struggling writer feel empowered in any writing situation, from state tests and college essays to emails and even text messaging. The essential principles of effective writing apply to all writing situations—only the formulas change.

Writing is not taught as a means to survive the expectations of rubrics, but rather as a deep-seated process that engages and empowers the struggling student. Gauging students' thinking processes and basic deficiencies in understanding the rules of language is the first step to promoting confidence. Teaching and reinforcing the "why" behind the principles of writing gives students the framework to build on. Reinforcing this knowledge using technology students are using outside school will only assist with engagement and growth in the writing process.

Writing becomes art when it's seen as a subjective and individualized endeavor. "Beauty in the eye of the beholder" should be the writer's motto, but only after understanding the principles of sound practices across genres and academic disciplines. Once those are in place, the larger frameworks can be effectively introduced. Allowing the struggling writer to study, collaborate, and showcase work online gives context to the writing process in motion, which leads to more sustained learning.

Whether planning, organizing, drafting, or revising, online writing programs are being developed to assist students with graphic organizers, mapping, and translating ideas. As this generation becomes more proficient at typing and tapping messages into word processors and tablets, these programs will feel more comfortable for the struggling writer who only handwrites in school. Speech-to-text programs also assist the struggling writer, particularly those with more confidence in expressing ideas in conversation. Finally, technology allows students to master structure with the cut or copy-paste options to shift ideas around rather than having to rewrite sections of text.

Courses of study on the writing process should begin and end with a digital portfolio that showcases a progression of skills, reflections, and principles learned. While the current model of education has students moving from grade level to grade level without a systemic scaffolding of fundamentals learned and drafted in practice sessions, a quick fix would be to offer a digital forum where work can be stored and shared with peers and teachers as the student progresses.

POINTS TO REMEMBER

- *Designing lessons that incorporate writing principles within these online genres is a practical solution for the struggling writer to practice and model what is learned in school with common communication outside the classroom.*
- *When typing, writing occurs in sequences, or bursts of activity, when the writer produces words before distinct pauses to think further about the writing task or process what was just written. The burst lengths are shorter depending on age, ability to type, or language impairments.*
- *Word processing enables the struggling writer to more easily transcribe and revise, streamline collaboration during different stages of the writing process, and share work on a global scale using the Internet.*
- *First and fifth graders who communicated with one another on a blog developed new literacies, and were more eager to offer instructional strategies of these literacies to peers and teachers.*
- *Audience and writing purposes are expanding due to digital composition tools that incorporate genres, modes, language, and platforms. This, along with an expansion of education into a multitude of arenas—public, private, international, informal—has further magnified the evolution of writing for varying needs.*

References

Adkins, A. (2013). *Effective strategies for teaching writing to struggling readers*. Retrieved from https://hubpages.com/education/Strategies-forTeaching-Writing-to-Struggling-Readers.

Alber, R. (2016). 4 strategies for teaching students how to revise. *Edutopia*. Retrieved from https://www.edutopia.org/blog/4-strategies-teaching-kids-how-revise-rebecca-alber.

Alves, R. A., Branco, M., Castro, S. L., & Olive, T. (2012). Effects of handwriting skill, output modes, and gender on fourth graders' pauses, language bursts, fluency, and quality. In V. W. Berninger (Ed.), *Past, present, and future contributions of cognitive writing research to cognitive psychology* (pp. 389–402). New York: Psychology Press.

Annenberg Foundation. (2017). *Mission and history*. Retrieved from https://www.learner.org/about/history.html.

Aukerman, M. (2013). Rereading comprehension pedagogies: Toward a dialogic teaching ethic that honors student sense making. *Dialogic Pedagogy: An International Online Journal*, 1. Retrieved from http://dpj.pitt.edu.

Aull, L. L., & Lancaster, Z. (2014). Linguistic markers of stance in early and advanced academic writing: A corpus-based comparison. *Written Communication*, 31, 151–183. doi:10.1177/0741088314527055.

Baltar, M. (2012). *Radio escolar: Gêneros textuais e letramento radiofônico na escola*. São Paulo, Brazil: Skoob.

Bazerman, C. (2016). What do sociocultural studies of writing tell us about learning to write? In C. MacArthur, S. Graham, & J. Fitzgerald (Eds.), *Handbook of writing research* (2nd ed.) (pp. 11–23). New York/London: The Guilford Press.

Beach, R., Newell, G., & VanDerHeide, J. (2016). A sociocultural perspective on writing development: Toward an agenda for classroom research on students' use of social practices. In C. MacArthur, S. Graham, & J. Fitzgerald (Eds.), *Handbook of writing research* (2nd ed.) (pp. 88–101). New York/London: The Guilford Press.

Beck, I. L., & Beck, M. E. (2012). *Making sense of phonics: The hows and whys.* New York: Guilford.

Behymer, A. (2003). Kindergarten writing workshop. *The Reading Teacher*, 57(1), 85–88. Retrieved from https://eric.ed.gov/?id=EJ674449.

Berninger, V. W. (2015). *Interdisciplinary frameworks for schools: Best professional practices for serving the needs of all students.* Washington, DC: American Psychological Association.

Berninger, V., Lee, Y., Abbott, R., & Breznitz, Z. (2013). Teaching children with dyslexia to spell in a reading-writers' workshop. *Annals of Dyslexia*, 63, 1–24. doi:10.1007/s11881-011-0054-0.

Berninger, V., & Niedo, J. (2014). Individualizing instruction for students with oral and written language difficulties. In J. Mascolo, D. Flanagan, & V. Alfonso (Eds.), *Essentials of planning, selecting and tailoring intervention: Addressing the needs of unique learners* (pp. 3–55). New York: Wiley.

Bowe, J., & Gore, J. (2017). Reassembling professional development: The case for quality teacher rounds. *Teacher and Teaching*, 23(3), 352–366. Retrieved from https://eric.ed.gov/?id=EJ1125327.

Browder, D., Wood, L., Thompson, J., & Ribuffo, C. (2014). *Evidence-based practices for students with severe disabilities (Document No. IC-3).* Retrieved from http://ceedar.education.ufl.edu/wp-content/uploads/2014/09/IC3_FINAL_03-03-15.pdf.

Bruning, R., & Kauffman, D. (2016). Self-efficacy beliefs and motivation in writing development. In C. MacArthur, S. Graham, & J. Fitzgerald (Eds.), *Handbook of writing research* (2nd ed.) (pp. 160–173). New York/London: The Guilford Press.

Bubb, S. (2013). Developing from within: Towards a new model of staff development. *Professional Development Today*, 15(1), 13–19. Retrieved from http://connection.ebscohost.com/c/articles/85830135/developing-from-within-towards-new-model-staff-development.

Butler, J. A., & Britt, M. A. (2011). Investigating instruction for improving revision of argumentative essays. *Written Communication*, 28(1), 70–96. doi:10.1177/0741088310387891.

Camp, H. (2012). The psychology of writing development—And its implications for assessment. *Assessing Writing*, 17, 92–105. doi.org/10.1016/j.asw.2012.01.002.

Calkins, L. (n.d.). Up the ladder: *Accessing grades 3–6 writing units of study* (Series Overview). Retrieved from http://www.heinemann.com/shared/online resources/e09658/utloverview.pdf?hsCtaTracking=33988c8d-5176-45f7-8686d35767c8f0f4%7C6636baa6d74f-4ced-af0e-c8debbb081eb.

Calkins, Lucy. (2016). *Remodeling the workshop: Lucy Calkins on writing instruction today*, Interview by Anthony Rebora. Retrieved from https://www.edweek.org.

Cannon, J., Swoszowski, N., Gallagher, P., & Easterbrooks, S. (2012). A program evaluation of an inclusive model for training pre-service general education teachers to work with students with special needs. *Journal of American Special Education Professionals*, Spring/Summer, 34–36. Retrieved from http://files.eric.ed.gov/fulltext/EJ1135618.pdf.

Center for the Collaborative Classroom. (2017). *Being a writer research.* Retrieved from https://www.collaborativeclassroom.org/research-being-a-writer.

Cho, K., & MacArthur, C. (2011). Learning by reviewing. *Journal of Educational Psychology*, 103, 73–84. Retrieved from https://eric.ed.gov/?id=EJ933615.

City, E., Elmore, R., Fiarman, S., & Teitel, L. (2010). *Instructional rounds in education: A network approach to improving teaching and learning.* Cambridge, MA: Harvard Education Press.

Colwell, C., MacIsaac, D., Tichenor, M., Heins, B., & Piechura, K. (2014). District and university perspectives on sustaining professional development schools: Do the NCATE standards matter? *The Professional Educator*, 38(2). Retrieved from https://eric.ed.gov/?id=EJ1048336.

Common Core State Standards. (2017). *About the standards.* Retrieved from http://www.corestandards.org/about-the-standards/.

Connelly, V., & Dockrell, J. (2016). Writing development and instruction for students with learning disabilities. In C. MacArthur, S. Graham, & J. Fitzgerald (Eds.), *Handbook of writing research* (pp. 211–226). New York: The Guilford Press.

Connelly, V., Dockrell, J. E., Walter, K., & Critten, S. (2012). Predicting the quality of composition and written language bursts from oral language, spelling, and handwriting skills in children with and without specific language impairment. *Written Communication, 29*, 278–302. doi:10.1177/0741088312451109.

Cook, B., & Cook, S. (2013). Unraveling evidence-based practices in special education. *Journal of Special Education*, 47(2), 71–82. doi:10.1177/0022466911420877.

Cook, B., Buysse, V., Klingner, J., Landrum, T., McWilliam, R., Tankersley, M., & Test, D. (2015). CEC's standards for classifying the evidence base practices in special education. *Remedial and Special Education*, 36(4), 220–234. doi:10.1177/0741932514557271.

Cook, B. G., & Odom, S. L. (2013). *Evidence based practices and implementation science in special education.* Retrieved from https://eric.ed.gov/?id=EJ1013632.

Cook, B., & Smith, G. (2012). Leadership and instruction: Evidence-based practices in special education. In J. B. Crockett, B. S. Billingsley, & M. L. Boscardin (Eds.), *Handbook of leadership in special education* (pp. 281–296). London, England: Routledge.

Cook, B., Smith, G., & Tankersley, M. (2012). Evidence-based practices in education. In K. Harris, T. Urdan, & S. Graham (Eds.), *American psychological association educational psychology handbook* (Vol. 1, pp. 495–528). Washington, DC. American Psychological Association. doi:10.1037/13273–017.

Costa, L. J., Ahmad, U., Edwards, C., Vanselous, S., Yerby, D. C., & Hooper, S. R. (2013). The writing side. In B. Miller, P. McCardle, & R. Long (Eds.), *Teaching reading and writing: Improving instruction and student achievement* (pp. 21–35). Baltimore: Paul H. Brookes.

Council for Exceptional Children. (2014). *Council for exceptional children: Standards for evidence-based practices in special education.* Retrieved from http://www.cec.sped.org/sitecore/shell/Controls/Rich%20Text%20Editor/~/media/F0A71BB0DEBD44ADBEF9628254A84F88.ashx.

Council for Exceptional Children's Interdivisional Research Group (2014). *Evidence-based special education in the context of scarce evidence-based practices.* doi:10.1177/0040059914551921.

Council of Writing Program Administrators, National Council of Teachers of English, and National Writing Project (2011). *Framework for success in postsecondary writing*. Urbana, IL: Authors.

Crinon, J. (2012). The dynamics of writing and peer review in elementary school. *Journal of Writing Research*, 4(2), 121–54. Retrieved from https://doaj.org/article/529ea929764f4b56bacf47e87af3bc1d.

Crossley, S. A., Roscoe, R., & McNamara, D. S. (2014). What is successful writing? An investigation into the multiple ways writers can write successful essays. *Written Communication*, 31, 184–214. doi:10.1177/0741088314526354.

Culham, R. (2011). *6+1 Traits of writing: The complete guide for the primary grades*. New York: Scholastic, Inc.

Cusumano, D. L., Algozzine, K., & Algozzine, B. (2014). Multi-tiered system of supports for effective inclusion in elementary schools. In J. McLeskey, N. L. Waldron, F. Spooner, & B. Algozzine (Eds.), *Handbook of effective inclusive schools: Research and practice* (pp. 197–209). New York: Routledge.

De La Paz, S., Ferretti, R., Wissinger, D., Yee, L., & MacArthur, C. (2012). Adolescents' disciplinary use of evidence, argumentative strategies, and organizational structure in writing about historical controversies. *Written Communication*, 29(4), 412–454. doi:10.1177/0741088312461591.

De La Paz, S., & Sherman, C. (2013). Revising strategy instruction in inclusive settings: Effects for English learners and novice writers. *Learning Disabilities Research & Practice*, 28(3). 129–141. Retrieved from http://onlinelibrary.wiley.com/doi/10.1111/ldrp.12011/full.

Demonte, J. (2013). *High-quality professional development for teachers: Supporting teacher training to improve student learning*. Center for American Progress: Washington, D.C. Retrieved from https://cdn.americanprogress.org/wpcontent/uploads/2013/07/DeMonteLearning4Teacher s-1.pdf.

Deshler, D. D., & Cornett, J. (2012). Leading to improve teacher effectiveness: Implications for practice, reform, research, and policy. In J. B Crockett, B. S. Billingsley, & M. L. Boscardin (Eds.), *Handbook of leadership and administration for special education* (pp. 239–259). New York: Taylor & Francis.

de Milliano, I., van Gelderen, A., & Sleegers, P. (2012). Patterns of cognitive self-regulation of adolescent struggling writers. *Written Communication*, 29(3), 303–325. doi:10.1177/0741088312450275.

Desimone, L. M., & Pak, K. (2017). Instructional coaching as high-quality professional development. *Theory into Practice*, 56(1), 3–12. doi:10.1080/00405841.2016.1241947.

DiPardo, A., Storms, B. A., & Selland, M. (2011). Seeing voices: Assessing writerly stance in the NWP Analytic Writing Continuum. *Assessing Writing*, 16, 170–88. Retrieved from https://www.nwp.org/cs/public/print/resource/3960.

Dockrell, J., Lindsay, G., & Connelly, V. (2009). The impact of specific language impairment on adolescents' written text. *Exceptional Children*, 75(4), 427–46. doi:10.1177/001440290907500403.

Duffy, W. (2014). Collaboration (in) theory: Reworking the social turn's conversational imperative. *College English*, 76(5), 416–435. Retrieved from http://ezproxy.neu.edu/login?url=https://search-proquestcom.ezproxy.neu.edu/docview/1518535076?accountid=12826.

Duke University. (2017). *Introduction to evidence based practice*. Retrieved from http://guides.mclibrary.duke.edu/c.php?g=158201&p=1036068.

Dyson, A. H. (2013). *ReWRITING the basics: Literacy learning in children's cultures*. New York: Teachers College Press.

Earley, P., & Porritt, V. (2014). Evaluating the impact of professional development: The need for a student-focused approach. *Professional Development in Education*, 40(1), 112–129. doi:10.1080/19415257.2013.798741.

Ellis, E. S., Worthington, L. A., & Larkin, M. J. (1994). *Effective teaching principles and the design of quality tools for educators*. A commissioned paper for the National Center to Improve the Tools for Education (NCITE). University of Oregon, Eugene, OR. Retrieved from http://files.eric.ed.gov/fulltext/ED386854.pdf.

Ennis, R., Jolivette, K., Terry, N., Frederick, L., & Alberto, P. (2015). Class-wide teacher implementation of self-regulated strategy development for writing with students with E/BD in a residential facility. *Journal of Behavioral Education*, 24, 88–111. Retrieved from https://eric.ed.gov/?id=EJ1052708.

Erstad, O. (2013). *Digital learning lives: Trajectories, literacies, and schooling*. New York: Peter Lang.

Fayol, M., Alamargot, D., & Berninger, V. (2012). *Translation of thought to written text while composing*. New York: Psychology Press.

Ferretti, R. P., & Fan, Y. (2016). Argumentative writing. In C. MacArthur, S. Graham, & J. Fitzgerald (Eds.), *Handbook of writing research* (2nd ed.) (pp. 301–315). New York/London: The Guilford Press.

Ferretti, R. P., & Lewis, W. E. (2013). Best practices in teaching argumentative writing. In S. Graham, C. A. MacArthur, & J. Fitzgerald (Eds.), *Best practices in writing instruction* (2nd ed.) (pp. 113–40). New York: Guilford Press.

Fettig, A. (2013). *Social skills training (SST) fact sheet*. Retrieved from http://autismpdc.fpg.unc.edu/sites/autismpdc.fpg.unc.edu/files/Social_Skills_Training_factsheet.pdf.

Flanagan, S., & Bouck, E. (2015). Mapping out the details: Supporting struggling writers' written expression with concept mapping. *Preventing School Failure*, 59(4), 244–252. doi:10.1080/1045988X.2014.933400.

Fleming, N. (2012). NAEP shows most students lack writing proficiency. *Education Week*. Retrieved from http://www.edweek.org/ew/articles/2012/09/14/04naep.h32.html.

Fountas, I. C., & Pinnell, G. S. (2001). *Guiding readers and writers: Teaching comprehension, genre, and content literacy*. New York: Heinemann.

Fu, D., & Shelton, N. (2007). Including students with special needs in a writing workshop. *National Council of Teachers of English*, 84(4), 325–336. Retrieved from http://www.imoberg.com/files/Including_Students_w_Special_Needs_in_Writing_Workshop_207_.pdf.

Gallagher, H. A., Woodworth, K. R., & Arshan, N. A. (2015). *Impact of the National Writing Project's College-Ready Writers Program on teachers and students*. Retrieved from https://www.sri.com/sites/default/files/publications/sri-crwp-research-brief_nov-2015-final.pdf.

Geeraerts, K., Tynjala, P., Heikkinen, H., Markkanen, I., Pennanen, M., & Gijbels, D. (2015). Peer-group mentoring as a toll for teacher development. *European Journal of Teacher Education*, 38(3), 358–377. doi:10.1080/19415257.2013.798741.

Gersten, R., Fuchs, L. S., Compton, D., Coyne, M., Greenwood, C., & Innocenti, M. S. (2005). Quality indicators for group experimental and quasi-experimental research in special education. *Exceptional Children*. doi:10.1177/001440290507100202.

Gilbert, J. & Graham, S. (2010). Teaching writing to elementary students in grades 4 to 6: A national survey. *Elementary School Journal*, 110, 494–518. doi:10.1086/651193.

Golley, A. (2015). *Teaching writing for students with learning disabilities in an inclusive classroom setting: A curriculum development project*. Retrieved from http://digitalcommons.brockport.edu/cgi/viewcontent.cgi?article=1282&context=surc.

Graham, S., Bollinger, A., Booth Olson, C., D'Aoust, C., MacArthur, C., McCutchen, D., & Olinghouse, N. (2012). *Teaching elementary school students to be effective writers*. Retrieved from https://ies.ed.gov/ncee/wwc/Docs/PracticeGuide/writing_pg_062612.pdf.

Graham, S., & Harris, K. R. (2016). A path to better writing: evidence-based practices in the classroom. *The Reading Teacher*, 69(4), 359–365. doi:10.1002/trtr.1432.

Graham, S., Harris, K., & Chambers, A. (2016). Evidence-based practice and writing instruction: A review of reviews. In C. MacArthur, S. Graham, & J. Fitzgerald (Eds.), *Handbook of writing research* (2nd ed.) (pp. 211–226). New York: The Guilford Press.

Graham, S., Harris, K. R., & McKeown, D. (2013). The writing of students with LD and a metaanalysis of SRSD writing intervention studies: Redux. In H. L. Swanson, K. Harris, & S. Graham (Eds.), *The handbook of learning disabilities* (2nd ed.) (pp. 405–38). New York: The Guilford Press.

Graham, S., McKeown, D., Kiuhara, S., & Harris, K. R. (2012). A meta-analysis of writing instruction for students in the elementary grades. *Journal of Educational Psychology*, 104, 879–96. doi:10.1037/a0029185.

Graham, S., & Sandmel, K. (2011). The process approach: A meta-analysis. *The Journal Of Educational Research*, 104, 396–407. doi:10.1080/00220671.2010.488703.

Great Schools Partnership. (2016). *Evidence-based*. Retrieved from http://edglossary.org/evidence-based/.

Green, T., & Allen, M. (2015). Professional development urban schools: What do teachers say? *Journal of Inquiry and Action in Education*, 6(2), 53–56. Retrieved from http://digitalcommons.buffalostate.edu/jiae/vol6/iss2/5/.

Gwosdek, H. (2013). *William Lily's grammar of Latin in English: An introduction of the Eyght Partes of Speche, and the construction of the same*. Oxford, UK: Oxford University Press.

Hanski, M. (2014). *What to be a better writer? Read more*. Retrieved from http://www.huffingtonpost.com/mike-hanski/read-more_b_5192754.html.

Harn, B., Parisi, D., & Stoolmiller, M. (2013). Balancing fidelity with flexibility and fit: What do we really know about fidelity of implementation in schools? *Exceptional Children*, 79, 181–93. doi: 10.1177/001440291307900204.

Harris, K., & Graham, S. (2013). An adjective is a word hanging down from a noun: Learning to write and students with learning disabilities. *Annals of Dyslexia*, 63, 65–79. Retrieved from https://www.ncbi.nlm.nih.gov/pubmed/21993603.

Harris, K. R., Graham, S., & Atkins, M. (2015). Tier 2, Teacher implemented writing strategies instruction following practice-based professional development. *Contemporary Educational Psychology*, 40, 5–16. doi:10.1016/j.cedpsych.2014.02.003.

Hawkins, J., Ginty, E., Kurzman, K. L., Leddy, D., Miller, J., Wiggins, G., & Wilbur., D. (2008). *Writing for understanding: Using backward design to help all students write effectively*. Burlington, VT: Vermont Writing Collaborative.

Hawkins, L. K., & Razali, A. B. (2012). A tale of 3 P's—Penmanship, product, and process: 100 years of elementary writing instruction. *Language Arts*, 89(5), 305–17. Retrieved from http://www.jstor.org/stable/41804351.

Hayes-Skelton, S., Roemer, L., Orsillo, S., & Borkovec, T. (2013). A contemporary view of applied relaxation for generalized anxiety disorder. *Cognitive Behaviour Therapy*, 42, 292–302. Retrieved from https://www.ncbi.nlm.nih.gov/pmc/articles/PMC3797858/.

Heinemann. (2017). *Up the ladder units overview*. Retrieved from http://www.hein emann.com/unitsofstudy/uptheladder/default.aspx#overview.

Hiebert, E. (2012). The Common Core State Standards and text complexity. In M. Hougen & S. Smartt (Eds.), *Fundamentals of literacy instruction & assessment pre-K-6* (pp. 111–120). Baltimore, MD: Brookes.

Holzberger, D., Philipp, A., & Kunter, M. (2013). How teachers' self-efficacy is related to instructional quality: A longitudinal analysis. *Journal of Educational Psychology*, 105, 774–786. Retrieved from https://eric.ed.gov/?id=EJ1054510.

Horner, R. H., Carr, E. G., Halle, J., McGee, G., Odom, S., & Wolery, M. (2005). *The use of single subject research to identify evidence-based practice in special education*. Retrieved from https://eric.ed.gov/?id=EJ696782.

Hudson, R. (2016). Grammar instruction. In C. MacArthur, S. Graham, & J. Fitzgerald (Eds.), *Handbook of writing research* (2nd ed.) (pp. 288–300). New York/London: The Guilford Press.

International Literacy Association. (2017). *The writing process*. Retrieved from http://www.readwritethink.org/professional-development/strategy-guides/imple mentingwriting-process-30386.html.

Johnson, E., Hancock, C., Carter, D., & Pool, J. (2012). Self-regulated strategy development as a tier 2 writing intervention. *Hamill Institute on Disabilities*, 48(4), 218–222. doi:10.1177/1053451212462880.

Keene, E. (2012). "What matters most in literacy teaching and learning" report. Retrieved from http://mosaicliteracy.com/docs/what_matters_most.pdf.

Keys to Literacy. (n.d.). *Literacy professional development for K–12 educators*. Retrieved from https://keystoliteracy.com/.

Kissel, B. T., & Miller, E. T. (2015). Reclaiming power in the Writers' Workshop. *Reading Teacher*, 69(1), 77–86. doi:10.1002/trtr.1379.

Kiuhara, S. A., O'Neill, R. E., Hawken, L. S., & Graham, S. (2012). The effectiveness of teaching 10th-grade students STOP, AIMS, AND DARE for planning and drafting persuasive text. *Exceptional Children*, 78, 335–355. doi:10.1177/001440291207800305.

Krasnoff, B. (2015). *What the research says about class size, professional development, and recruitment, induction, and retention of highly qualified teachers:*

A compendium of the evidence on title-II, part A, program-funded strategies. Retrieved from http://files.eric.ed.gov/fulltext/ED558138.pdf.

Kretlow, A., & Helf, S. (2013). Teacher implementation of evidence-based practices in tier 1: A national survey. *Teacher Education and Special Education*, 36(3), 167–185. doi:10.1177/0888406413489838.

Lacina, J., & Collins Block, C. (2012). Progressive writing instruction: Empowering school leaders and teachers. *Voices from the Middle*, 19, 10–17. Retrieved from https://eric.ed.gov/?id=EJ976255.

Lauer, P., Christopher, D., Firpo-Triplett, R., & Buchting, F. (2014). The impact of short-term professional development on participant outcomes: A review of the literature. *Professional Development in Education*, 40(2), 207–227. doi:10.1080/19415257.2013.776619.

Lee, A. (n.d.). *Every student succeeds act (ESSA): What you need to know.* Retrieved from https://www.understood.org/en/school-learning/your-childs-rights/basicsabout-childs-rights/every-student-succeeds-act-essa-what-you-need-to-know.

Lee, W., Lee, M. -J., & Bong, M. (2014). Testing interest and self-efficacy as predictors of academic self-regulation and achievement. *Contemporary Educational Psychology*, 29, 86–99. doi:10.1016/j.cedpsych.2014.02.002.

Leu, D., Slomp, D., Zawilinski, L., & Corrigan, J. (2016). Writing research through a new literacies lens. In C. MacArthur, S. Graham, & J. Fitzgerald (Eds.), *Handbook of writing research* (2nd ed.) (pp. 41–56). New York/London: The Guilford Press.

Luzón, M. J. (2013). Public communication of science in blogs: Recontextualized scientific discourse for a diversified audience. *Written Communication*. Retrieved from http://journals.sagepub.com/doi/abs/10.1177/0741088313493610.

MacArthur, C. (2016). Instruction in evaluation and revision. In C. MacArthur, S. Graham, & J. Fitzgerald (Eds.), *Handbook of writing research* (2nd ed.) (pp. 24–40). New York/London: The Guilford Press.

MacArthur, C., Graham, S., & Fitzgerald, J. (2016). Introduction. In C. MacArthur, S. Graham, & J. Fitzgerald (Eds.), *Handbook of writing research* (2nd ed.) (pp. 1–10). New York/London: The Guilford Press.

MacArthur, C. A., Philippakos, Z. A., & Ianetta, M. (2015). Self-regulated strategy instruction in college developmental writing. *Journal of Educational Psychology*. Retrieved from http://dx.doi.org/10.1037/edu0000011.

Marrongelle, K., Sztajn, P., & Smith, M. (2013). Scaling up professional development in an era of common core state standards. *Journal of Teacher Education*, 64(3), 202–218. doi:10.1177/0022487112473838.

Marshall, K., Karvonen, M., Yell, M., Lowry, A., Drasgow, E., & Seaman, M. (2013). Project ReSpecT: Toward an evidence-based mentoring model for induction teachers. *Journal of Disability Policy Studies*. Sage Publications, 24(3), 127–136. doi:10.1177/1044207313480837.

Marzano, R. J., Pickering, D. J., & Pollock, J. E. (2001). *Classroom instruction that works*. Association for Supervision and Curriculum Development. Alexandria, VA: ASCD.

Massachusetts Department of Elementary and Secondary Education. (2017). *Curriculum and instruction: Writing standards in action project*. Retrieved from http://www.doe.mass.edu/candi/wsa/.

Mather, N. & Wendling, B. J. (2012). *Essentials of dyslexia: Assessment & intervention.* Hoboken, NJ: Wiley & Sons.

McCarrier, A., Pinnell, G. S., & Fountas, I. C. (2000). *Interactive writing.* Portsmouth, NH: Heinemann.

McCarthey, S. J., & Mkhize, D. (2013). Teachers' orientations towards writing. *Journal of Writing Research,* 5(1), 1–33. Retrieved from http://www.jowr.org/articles/vol5_1/JoWR_2013_vol5_nr1_McCarthey_Mkhize.pdf.

Mercer, N., & Howe, C. (2012). Explaining the dialogic processes of teaching and learning: The value and potential of sociocultural theory. *Learning, Culture, and Social Interaction,* 1, 12–21. Retrieved from PII:S2210656112000049.

Mills, Geoffrey (2002). *Action research: A guide for the teacher researcher.* Upper Saddle River, NJ: Merrill Prentice Hall.

Moore, N., & MacArthur, C. A. (2012). The effects of being a reader and of observing readers on fifth grade students' argumentative writing and revising. *Reading and Writing,* 25, 1449–1478. Retrieved from https://eric.ed.gov/?id=EJ969921.

Morin, A. (2014). At a glance: Classroom accommodations for dysgraphia. *Understood for learning and attention issues.* Retrieved from https://www.understood.org/en/schoollearning/partnering-with-childsschool/instructional-strategies/at-a-glance-classroomaccommodations-for-dysgraphia.

Myhill, D. A., Jones, S. M., Lines, H., & Watson, A. (2012). Re-thinking grammar: The impact of embedded grammar teaching on students' writing and students' metalinguistic understanding. *Research Papers in Education,* 27, 139–166. doi:10.1080/02671522.2011.637640.

National Center for Education Statistics. (2012). *The Nation's Report Card: Writing 2011* (No. NCES 2012–470). Washington, DC: Author. Retrieved from https://nces.ed.gov/nationsreportcard/pdf/main2011/2012470.pdf.

National Council of Teacher of English. (2017). *Resources and professional learning.* Retrieved from http://www.ncte.org/Default.aspx.

National Writing Project. (2015). *Joyous learning: 2015 National writing project annual report.* Retrieved from www.ar15.nwp.org.

National Writing Project. (2017). *About the national writing project.* Retrieved from https://www.nwp.org/cs/public/print/doc/about.csp.

Nelson, C. A. (2015). *Building Literacy Capacity: The conditions for effective standards implementation.* National Center for Literacy Education/National Council of Teachers of English. Retrieved from http://www.ncte.org/library/NCTEFiles/NCLE/2015-NCLE-Report-Framing.pdf.

NORC (2013). *Getting on track early for school success: Research and practice in the field of early literacy learning.* Retrieved from http://www.norc.org/Research/Projects/Pages/getting-on-track-early-for-school-success-an-assessment-system-to-support-effective-instruction.aspx.

Olinghouse, N., & Wilson, J. (2013). The relationship between vocabulary and writing quality in three genres. *Reading & Writing: An Interdisciplinary Journal,* 26, 45–66. doi:10.1007/s11145012–9392–5.

Olinghouse, N. G., Zheng, J., & Morlock, L. (2012). State writing assessment: Inclusion of motivational factors in writing tasks. *Reading and Writing Quarterly,* 28, 97–119. doi:10.1080/10573569.2012.632736.

Osten, M., & Gidseg, E. The hows and whys of peer mentoring. *Rethinking Schools*. Retrieved from http://rethinkingschools.aidcvt.com/special_reports/quality_teach ers/peersd.shtml.

Pearson Education. (2015). *MCAS Resource Center: English language arts practice tests*. Retrieved from http://mcas.pearsonsupport.com/tutorial/practice-tests-ela/.

Philippakos, Z. A., & MacArthur, C. A. (2016). The effects of giving feedback on the persuasive writing of fourth- and fifth-grade students. *Reading Research Quarterly*, 51(4), 419–433. doi:10.1002/rrq.149.

Pifarré, M., & Li, L. (2012). Teaching how to learn with a wiki in primary education: What classroom interaction can tell us. *Learning, Culture and Social Interaction*, 1(2), 102–113. Retrieved from http://hdl.handle.net/10459.1/46994.

Pigg, S., Grabill, J. T., Brunk-Chavez, B., Moore, J. L., Rosinski, P., & Curran, P. G. (2014). Ubiquitous writing, technologies, and the social practice of literacies of coordination. *Written Communication*, 31(1), 91–117. doi:10.1177/0741088313514023.

Proske, A., & Kapp, F. (2013). Fostering topic knowledge: Essential for academic writing. *Reading and Writing*, 26, 1337–1352. doi:10.1007/s11145-012-9421-4.

Puddy, R. W., & Wilkins, N. (2011). Understanding evidence part 1: Best available research evidence. A guide to the continuum of evidence of effectiveness. Atlanta, GA: Centers for Disease Control and Prevention. Retrieved from https://www.cdc. gov/violenceprevention/pdf/understanding_evidence-a.pdf.

Purcell, K., Heaps, A., Buchanan, J., & Friedrich, L. (2013). How teachers are using technology at home and in their classrooms. Retrieved from http://www.pewinter net.org/2013/02/28/how-teachers-are-using-technology-at-homeand-in-their-class rooms/.

Ray, Katie Wood. (2015). *The teacher you want to be*. Portsmouth, NH: Heinemann.

Roscoe, R. D., & McNamara, D. S. (2013). Writing Pal: Feasibility of an intelligent writing strategy tutor in the high school classroom. *Journal of Educational Psychology*, 105, 1010–1025. Retrieved from https://asu.pure.elsevier.com/en/ publications/writing-palfeasibility-of-an-intelligent-writing-strategy-tutor-.

Samuels, C. A. (2016). Number of U.S. students in special education ticks upward. Retrieved from http://www.edweek.org/ew/articles/2016/04/20/number-of-us-students-in-specialeducation.html.

Scheeler, M., Budin, S., & Markelz, A. (2016). The role of teacher preparation in promoting evidence-based practice in schools. *Learning Disabilities: A Contemporary Journal*, 14(2), 171–187. Retrieved from http://www.ldw-ldcj.org/index.php/ manuscriptsubmission/64-therole-of-teacher-preparation-in-promoting-evidence-based-practice-in-schools.html.

Schultz, K., Hull, G., & Higgs, J. (2016). After writing, after school. In C. MacArthur, S. Graham, & J. Fitzgerald (Eds.), *Handbook of writing research* (2nd ed.) (pp. 102–115). New York/London: The Guilford Press.

Siegle, D. (2015). *Single subject research*. Retrieved from http://researchbasics.edu cation.uconn.edu/single-subject-research/.

Shanahan, T. (2016). Relationships between reading and writing development. In C. MacArthur, S. Graham, & J. Fitzgerald (Eds.), *Handbook of writing research* (2nd ed.) (pp. 194–210). New York/London: The Guilford Press.

Shaywitz, S. (2005). *Overcoming dyslexia: A new and complete science-based program for reading problems at any level*. New York: Random House.

Shermis, M. D., & Burstein, J. (Eds.). (2013). *Handbook of automated essay evaluation: Current applications and new directions*. New York: Routledge.

Smartt, S. M., & Glaser, D. R. (2010). *Next STEPS in literacy instruction: Connecting assessments to effective interventions*. Baltimore, MD: Brookes.

Snowling, M. J., & Hulme, C. (2012). Annual research review: The nature and classification of reading disorders—a commentary on proposals for DSM-5. *Journal of Child Psychology and Psychiatry*, 53(5), 593–607. Retrieved from https://www.ncbi.nlm.nih.gov/pubmed/22141434.

Song, Y., & Ferretti, R. P. (2013). Teaching critical questions about argumentation through the revising process: Effects of strategy instruction on college students' argumentative essays. *Reading and Writing*, 26, 67–90. Retrieved from https://eric.ed.gov/?id=EJ991685.

Sornson, B. (2015). The effects of using the essential skills inventory on teacher perception of high-quality classroom instruction. *Preventing School Failure*, 59(3), 161–167. doi:10.1080/1045988X.2014.886551.

Stahl, M. C. & Dougherty Stahl, K. A. (2015). *Assessment for reading instruction* (3rd ed). New York: The Guilford Press.

Stone, C. A., Silliman, E. R., Ehren, B. J., & Wallach, G. P. (2014). *Handbook of language and literacy: Development and disorder* (2nd ed). New York, NY: Guilford Press.

Taft, R., & Mason, L. H. (2011). Examining effect of writing interventions: Highlighting results for students with primary disabilities other than learning disabilities. *Remedial and Special Education: Hammill Institute on Disabilities*, 32(5), 359–370. doi:10.1177/0741932510362242.

Teachers College Reading and Writing Project. (2016). Research base underlying the teachers college reading and writing workshop's approach to literacy instruction. Retrieved from http://readingandwritingproject.org/about/research-base.

Thompson, I. (2012). Planes of communicative activity in collaborative writing. *Changing English: Studies in Culture and Education*, 19(2), 209–220. Retrieved from https://eric.ed.gov/?id=EJ1109630.

Tolchinsky, L. (2016). From text to language and back: The emergence of written language. In C. MacArthur, S. Graham, & J. Fitzgerald (Eds.), *Handbook of writing research* (2nd ed.). (pp. 144–59) New York: The Guilford Press.

Troia, G. (2013). Writing instruction within a response-to-intervention framework. In Graham, S., MacAuthur, C., & Fitzgerald, J. (Eds.). *Best practices in writing instruction* (2nd ed). New York: The Guilford Press.

Troia, G. (2014). Evidence-based practices for writing instruction (Document No. IC-5). Retrieved from http://ceedar.education.ufl.edu/tools/innovation-configuration/.

Troia, G., & Olinghouse, N. (2013). The Common Core State Standards and evidence-based educational practices: The case of writing. *School Psychology Review*, 42, 343–357. Retrieved from https://eric.ed.gov/?id=ED566949.

Torrance, M. (2016). Understanding planning in text production. In C. MacArthur, S. Graham, & J. Fitzgerald (Eds.), *Handbook of writing research* (2nd ed.) (pp. 72–87). New York: The Guilford Press.

U.S. Department of Education. (2015). Every student succeeds act. Retrieved from https://www.ed.gov/essa?src=ft.

U.S. Department of Education. (n.d.). Every student succeeds act (ESSA). Retrieved from https://www.ed.gov/ESSA.

Vanassche, E. & Kelchermans, G. (2015). *A narrative analysis of a teacher educator's professional learning journey.* doi: 10.1080.02619768.2016.1187127.

van den Bergh, H., Rijlaarsdam, G., & van Steendam, E. (2016). Writing process theory: A functional dynamic approach. In C. MacArthur, S. Graham, & J. Fitzgerald (Eds.), *Handbook of writing research* (2nd ed.) (pp. 57–71). New York: The Guilford Press.

VanDerHeide, J., & Newell, G. E. (2013). Instructional chains as a method for examining the teaching and learning of argumentative writing in classrooms. *Written Communication*, 30, 300–329. doi:10.1177/0741088313491713.

Varner, L. K., Roscoe, R. D., & McNamara, D. S. (2013). Evaluative misalignment of 10th-grade student and teacher criteria for essay quality: An automated textual analysis. *Journal of Writing Research*, 5, 35–59. Retrieved from http://129.219.222.66/Publish/pdf/Varner_2013.pdf.

Vermont Writing Collaborative. (2016). Structure of the 2016 Writing for Understanding summer institute. Retrieved from http://www.vermontwritingcollaborative.org/WPDEV/wpcontent/uploads/2016/02/Structure-of-2016-Writing-for-Understanding-Summer-Institute.pdf.

Vermont Writing Collaborative. (2017a). Writing for understanding. Retrieved from http://www.vermontwritingcollaborative.org/WPDEV/our-approach/.

Vermont Writing Collaborative. (2017b). What is the "painted essay"? Retrieved from http://www.vermontwritingcollaborative.org/WPDEV/painted-essay/.

Wardle, E., & Roozen, K. (2012). Addressing multiple dimensions of writing development: Toward an ecological model of assessment. *Assessing Writing*, 17, 106–119. doi: 10.1016/j.asw.2012.01.001.

Warren, J. E. (2013). Rhetorical reading as a gateway to disciplinary literacy. *Journal of Adolescent and Adult Literacy*, 56(5), 391–399. Retrieved from https://eric.ed.gov/?id=EJ1009198.

Western Massachusetts Writing Project. (2017). *Western MA writing project.* Retrieved from https://www.umass.edu/wmwp/frontpage.

What Works Clearinghouse (2015). Procedures and standards handbook (Version 3.0). Retrieved from https://ies.ed.gov/ncee/wwc/Docs/ReferenceResources/wwc_scd_key_criteria_011017.pdf.

What Works Clearinghouse (2017). Scientific evidence. Retrieved from https://ies.ed.gov/ncee/wwc/WhatWeDo.

Wiggins, G., & McTighe, J. (1998). *Understanding by design.* Alexandria, VA: ASCD.

Wills, K. V., & Rice, R. (2013). *Eportfolio performance support systems: Constructing, presenting, and assessing portfolios.* Anderson, SC: Parlor Press.

Wood, C., Kemp, N., & Plester, B. (2013). *Text messaging and literacy: The evidence.* New York: Routledge.

Wright, P.W.D. (2004). The individuals with disabilities education improvement act of 2004. Retrieved from http://www.wrightslaw.com/idea/idea.2004.all.pdf.

Zawilinski, L. (2012). An exploration of a collaborative blogging approach to literacy and learning: A mixed method study. Unpublished doctoral dissertation, University of Connecticut, Storrs. Retrieved from https://pqdtopen.proquest.com/doc/1237997446.html?FMT=AI.

Zumbrunn, S., & Bruning, R. (2013). Improving the writing and knowledge of emergent writers: The effects of self-regulated strategy development. *Reading and Writing: An Interdisciplinary Journal*, 26, 91–110. Retrieved from https://eric.ed.gov/?id=EJ991683.

About the Authors

Nicholas D. Young, PhD, EdD

Dr. Nicholas D. Young has worked in diverse educational roles for more than twenty-eight years, serving as a principal, special education director, graduate professor, graduate program director, graduate dean, and longtime superintendent of schools. He was named the Massachusetts Superintendent of the Year, and he completed a distinguished Fulbright program focused on the Japanese educational system through the collegiate level. Dr. Young is the recipient of numerous other honors and recognitions including the General Douglas MacArthur Award for distinguished civilian and military leadership and the Vice Admiral John T. Hayward Award for exemplary scholarship. He holds several graduate degrees including a PhD in educational administration and an EdD in educational psychology.

Dr. Young has served in the U.S. Army and U.S. Army Reserves combined for over thirty-three years; and he graduated with distinction from the U.S. Air War College, the U.S. Army War College, and the U.S. Navy War College. After completing a series of senior leadership assignments in the U.S. Army Reserves as the commanding officer of the 287th Medical Company (DS), the 405th Area Support Company (DS), the 405th Combat Support Hospital, and the 399th Combat Support Hospital, he transitioned to his current military position as a faculty instructor at the U.S. Army War College in Carlisle, Pennsylvania. He currently holds the rank of colonel.

Dr. Young is also a regular presenter at state, national, and international conferences; and he has written many books, book chapters, and/or articles on various topics in education, counseling, and psychology. Some of his most recent books include *From Head to Heart: High Quality Teaching Practices in the Spotlight* (in-press); *Dog Tags to Diploma: Understanding and Addressing the Educational Needs of Veterans, Servicemembers, and their Families* (in-press); *From Cradle to Classroom: Identifying and Addressing the Educational Needs of Our Youngest Children,* (in-press); *Achieving Results: Maximizing Success in the Schoolhouse* (in-press); *Making the Grade: Promoting Positive Outcomes for Students with Learning Disabilities* (in-press); *Paving the Pathway for Educational Success: Effective Classroom Interventions for Students with Learning Disabilities* (in-press); *Floundering to Fluent: Reaching and Teaching the Struggling Student* (2018); *Emotions and Education: Promoting Positive Mental Health in Students with Learning* (2018); *From Lecture Hall to Laptop: Opportunities, Challenges, and the Continuing Evolution of Virtual Learning in Higher Education* (2017); *The Power of the Professoriate: Demands, Challenges, and Opportunities in 21st Century Higher Education* (2017); *To Campus with Confidence: Supporting a Successful Transition to College for Students with Learning Disabilities* (2017); *Educational Entrepreneurship: Promoting Public-Private Partnerships for the 21st Century* (2015); *Beyond the Bedtime Story: Promoting Reading Development during the Middle School Years* (2015); *Betwixt and Between: Understanding and Meeting the Social and Emotional Developmental Needs of Students During the Middle School Transition Years* (2014); *Learning Style Perspectives: Impact Upon the Classroom* (3rd ed., 2014); and *Collapsing Educational Boundaries from Preschool to PhD: Building Bridges Across the Educational Spectrum* (2013); *Transforming Special Education Practices: A Primer for School Administrators and Policy Makers* (2012); and *Powerful Partners in Student Success: Schools, Families and Communities* (2012). He has also co-authored several children's books to include the popular series *I am Full of Possibilities.*

Bryan Thors Noonan
Since stepping away from the news desk in 2006 after eight years as a reporter at three daily newspapers and a weekly magazine, Bryan Thors Noonan began designing award-winning scholastic writing programs at a Turnaround High School at Duval County Public Schools in Jacksonville, Florida. In August 2017, he became a reading and English language arts specialist for Duval County, where he began coaching educators teaching academic writing to more than 10,000 students across twenty-two high schools.

During his tenure in the classroom, Mr. Noonan developed a writing curriculum focused on the Florida state assessment standards, as well as a journalism program that has been celebrated by professional journalists for having some of the finest student writers in the nation. One of the competitions, which has spanned more than forty years at Jacksonville's major metropolitan newspaper, honored Mr. Noonan's efforts in the editorial page of *The Florida Times-Union*: "Noonan inspired a depth of writing quality among his students that has rarely been seen."

Over six years as newspaper advisor, Mr. Noonan's staff consistently swept news and opinion writing categories against the top-rated high schools in Northeast Florida. His staff writers were honored with more than seventy individual awards, including twenty-six first place finishes in a half-dozen writing categories, while winning Best Newspaper honors three years in a row at The Florida Times-Union High School Journalism Awards. Mr. Noonan's students also won more than a dozen national awards, including first-place finishes for feature writing and opinion pieces at the National Scholastic Press Association awards, Columbia Scholastic Press Awards, Scholastic Art and Writing Awards, and Arts for Life! competition.

Mr. Noonan's writing career began as a student at the University of Missouri School of Journalism. Before graduating in 2001 with an emphasis in news-editorial writing, he was named beat reporter for the Missouri baseball team at the Columbia Missourian. From there, Mr. Noonan went on to work at three publications covering education, health news, military affairs, and, finally, public safety, where Noonan won multiple awards for in-depth criminal investigations.

In 2016, Mr. Noonan self-published two workbooks entitled *Leaving Your Literary Legacy*, which guides students through his twelve principles of great writing. As a companion to the book, Noonan is building a website to encourage teens to submit original work based on his philosophies of writing. His website, lyll-online.com, also offers a writing class for students to practice targeted writing skills. Mr. Noonan is working toward building an independent publishing company to help young writers get their first books in print.

Kristen Bonanno-Sotiropoulos

Professor Bonanno-Sotiropoulos has worked in education for more than a dozen years. Her professional career within K–12 public education included roles as a special education teacher and special education administrator at the elementary and middle school levels before transitioning to higher education to teach undergraduate and graduate courses as an assistant professor of special education at Springfield College located in Springfield, Massachusetts.

Professor Bonanno-Sotiropoulos received her bachelor of science in liberal studies and elementary education with academic distinction as well as a master of science in moderate disabilities from Bay Path University. She is currently an EdD in educational leadership and supervision candidate at American International College, where she is focusing her research on evidence-based special education practices.

Professor Bonanno-Sotiropoulos has become a regular presenter at regional and national conferences, and she has coauthored a series of book chapters on the unique needs of struggling readers as well as on how higher education institutions can assist special needs students with making a successful transition to college. Her current research interests include effective instructional programs and practices that assist students with learning disabilities meet rigorous academic expectations at all academic levels from preschool to college.